Program Design and Development
for Gifted and Talented Students

The Authors

Frederick B. Tuttle, Jr., is Assistant Superintendent, Needham Public Schools, Massachusetts. He is a former university professor of education and an educational consultant in gifted education and written composition. Dr. Tuttle is the author of *Composition: A Media Approach, Gifted and Talented Students,* and *How to Prepare Students for Writing Tests;* the editor of *Fine Arts in the Curriculum;* and the coauthor of *Technical and Scientific Writing,* and *Characteristics and Identification of Gifted and Talented Students,* all published by NEA. He also developed the NEA multimedia program *Educating Gifted and Talented Students.*

Laurence A. Becker, a former high school English teacher, is an Educational Consultant in Creative Learning Environments. He leads workshops throughout the United States in creativity, filmmaking, and teacher training for work with gifted learners.

Joan A. Sousa is an elementary school principal in the East Greenwich (Rhode Island) Public Schools. A former classroom teacher, teacher of the gifted, and coordinator of gifted and talented programs, Mrs. Sousa also serves as a member and past chairperson of the Commissioner's Advisory Council on Gifted and Talented Education for the state of Rhode Island.

The Consultants

Dr. Paul D. Plowman, Consultant and Federal Integrative Education Project Director, California State Department of Education, Sacramento

Dr. Joseph S. Renzulli, Professor of Educational Psychology, School of Education, University of Connecticut, Storrs

Dr. Dorothy Sisk, Professor, Gifted Child Education, University of South Florida, Tampa

William G. Vassar, Consultant for Gifted and Talented, Connecticut State Department of Education, Hartford

The Advisory Panel

Dr. John A. Grossi, Director, Gifted and Talented, The Council for Exceptional Children, Reston, Virginia

Deanna M. Gutschow, ESEA Title IV-C Project Director, Gifted Writing Program, Whitefish Bay Schools, Wisconsin

J. Beatrice Hall, Consultant, Education of Gifted and Talented, Austin, Texas

William C. Morgan, teacher of Gifted and Talented, Plymouth High School, Plymouth, North Carolina

Judith M. Plummer, teacher, Gifted Education Program, Mitchell School, Woodbury, Connecticut

Program Design and Development
for Gifted and Talented Students

Third Edition

by Frederick B. Tuttle, Jr.
Laurence A. Becker
Joan A. Sousa

nea PROFESSIONAL LIBRARY
National Education Association
Washington, D.C.

Library of Congress Cataloging-in-Publication Data

Tuttle, Frederick B.
    Program design and development for gifted and talented students.

    Bibliography: p.
    1. Gifted children—Education—United States—
Curricula.   2. Curriculum planning—United States.
I. Becker, Laurence A.   II. Sousa, Joan.   III. Title.
LC3993.9.T874   1988   371.95   87-31565
ISBN 0-8106-0727-1

Acknowledgments

The following materials are reprinted with permission from the sources indicated: List of areas stressed in counseling components of programs for gifted and Roles of Involved Personnel from "Identification of Talented Students" by Philip A. Perrone et al., Guidance Institute for Talented Students, University of Wisconsin-Madison, n.d. Excerpts from *Classroom Ideas for Encouraging Thinking and Feeling* (including list of pupil behaviors and meanings from "Thinking-Feeling" model and activity from page 81) by Frank E. Williams; copyright © 1970 by D.O.K. Publishers, Inc. Illustration of Structure of the Intellect Model, with graphic modifications, from *The Nature of Human Intelligence* by J. P. Guilford; copyright © 1967 by McGraw-Hill Book Co. Excerpts from *The Enrichment Triad Model* by Joseph Renzulli (including Figure 1 from page 14, quotation from page 30, and "Prototype of a Type III Enrichment Activity in Social Science"); copyright © 1977 by Creative Learning Press, P.O. Box 320, Mansfield Center, Connecticut 06250. Excerpt from "Guidelines for Establishing and Evaluating Programs for Mentally Gifted Minors" by Paul D. Plowman, California State Department of Education, Sacramento, 1962. Two Phases of Program Development from "Procedures in Programming for Talented Students" by Phillip A. Perrone, Dana Morris-Jones, and Phyllis Post, Guidance Institute for Talented Students, University of Wisconsin-Madison, n.d. "Differentiating Curriculum for the Gifted and Talented" from pages 123-26 of *Providing Programs for the Gifted and Talented: A Handbook* by Sandra N. Kaplan (Ventura, Calif., 1974); reprinted by permission of the publisher, the National/State Leadership Training Institute on the Gifted and the Talented. "Masters and Ph.D. Programs in Gifted Education or with Emphasis in Gifted Education" prepared by the National/State Leadership Training Institute on the Gifted and the Talented, from the August 1979 N/S-LTI-G/T *Bulletin*. Program for Academically and Creatively Talented (PACT), Needham (Massachusetts) Public Schools. Project Prism, Foxborough (Massachusetts) Schools. "Management Plan for Individual and Small Group Investigations" from *A Guidebook for Developing Individualized Educational Programs for Gifted and Talented Students* by Joseph S. Renzulli and Linda H. Smith; copyright © 1979 by Creative Learning Press. Adaptation of activities based on the Structure of the Intellect Model developed by Donald Nasca, Bureau of Educational Field Services, State University of New York, College at Brockport, n.d.

CONTENTS

AUTHORS' PREFACE
TO THE THIRD EDITION

Upon review of the second edition of this book, we find two areas that warrant further attention. Consequently, the revisions for the third edition consist primarily of additional descriptions of programs for gifted and talented students and a description of the Pyramid Project being conducted in the Dallas/Fort Worth area under the leadership of the Gifted Students Institute for Research and Development.

This program is particularly noteworthy because of the systematic infusion of opportunities for gifted students in the regular classroom. While other models, such as the Advanced Skills Model, may easily be adapted for the regular classroom, the Pyramid Project is developing its approach in an ambitiously comprehensive manner, attempting to

> meet the needs of talented K-12 youngsters in all content areas and at all levels of ability, from the above-average to the highly gifted. No children will be excluded from any provision that meets their needs. (F, p. 160*)

With estimated funding of $3,500,000 over a five-year period, the Pyramid Project certainly calls for continued attention.

Other revisions include a concern with pullout programs (see "Misconception 6: Something is better than nothing," pp. 20–21) and an addition to Chapter 4, "Teacher Selection."

---

*Letters in parentheses refer to the Additional Resources for the Third Edition beginning on page 147.

INTRODUCTION

Program Design and Development for Gifted and Talented Students is the second book in NEA's multimedia program *Educating the Gifted and Talented,* which is designed to provide background information, supplementary materials, workshop activities, and discussion questions for (a) individuals preparing to work with gifted students, (b) teachers currently working with classes of gifted students, and (c) teachers with a few gifted students in their classes. The materials in this program are also intended to help administrators and parents concerned with issues involved in the education of the gifted.

The book's general format consists of three sections: (1) background information and ideas on major aspects of program design and development; (2) supplementary materials and examples for the interest and use of readers; and (3) a series of activities to help readers become involved with the topic(s) and to apply the ideas to their specific situations. Examples, related experiences, and commentary are provided throughout the text for interest as well as for illustration of ideas. Although the facts in the anecdotes and the case study are true, the names of persons involved have been changed to protect their privacy.

While the various areas of concern are presented sequentially, teachers and program developers are encouraged to move freely back and forth among them. When considering program development, for instance, specific characteristics of the gifted in the school population should be kept clearly in mind so that the strategies developed will build upon these characteristics rather than contradict them. If, for example, the aim is to design a program to develop general intellectual or creative abilities, it would be well to avoid a narrow, accelerated, content-oriented curriculum, the focus of which would be in opposition to the broad interests and probing curiosity characteristic of this population.

We gratefully acknowledge the many substantive contributions to this work by Margot Nicholas Parrot of Hancock, Maine, a parent of three highly gifted children and an adult with many gifts herself. We are grateful, too, for the comments of the teachers and administrators enrolled in the Gifted Institute during the spring of 1979, as well as for the comments of those teachers who worked with these materials in the fall of 1979.

We extend special thanks to Patricia Tuttle and Rosanne Becker for their extreme patience and endurance during the many writing sessions involved in the completion of this work.

Chapter 1
RATIONALE FOR SPECIAL PROVISION FOR GIFTED AND TALENTED STUDENTS

When we hear the term "gifted," many of us immediately envision brilliant students or precocious artists. Seldom, do we think of struggling individuals who feel out of place in school and society. Actually, the term encompasses all these individuals and others. All, however, have some common concerns, especially within most academic environments. Most gifted students possess particular characteristics not often addressed in classrooms. Indeed, such traits place not a few of these students at a disadvantage in many classes. In other words, they cannot benefit fully from their educational experiences unless some special provision is made to accommodate and build upon their characteristics. Therefore it is important to develop a clear understanding of the need for such provision as well as of the benefits it offers individual students, the schools, and, ultimately, society.

BENEFITS TO THE INDIVIDUAL

As Treffinger stated, "Gifted programming is an essential component of a school district's 'charge' to recognize and respond to individual differences, so that all students may have opportunities to reach their optimum personal and academic development" (Q, p. 50). Most statements of general educational goals contain the concept of differentiating instruction to meet individuals needs and abilities. Such a goal statement has, in fact, formed the basis for much work with handicapped students and the learning disabled. The same great need exists for the group called "gifted and talented." While these individuals differ greatly from each other, there are some general group characteristics that call for the formation of special programs to meet their needs and interests. Vassar has cited the following:

10

The gifted and talented need to:

- use, develop, and understand higher mental processes.
- interchange and dialogue with their intellectual peers (those with similar interests, talents, etc.).
- have the time, space, and staff necessary to assist in the development of their outstanding ability.
- understand, appreciate, and study the diversity among individuals.
- have available an appropriate identification process and access to specialized counseling.
- learn to develop life styles commensurate with their particular profile of abilities and talents.
- have the opportunity to assess their unique talents and interests. (17)*

Characteristics and Identification of Gifted and Talented Students discusses the characteristics of the gifted. Some of these traits such as the following are often ignored or even penalized within the regular classroom setting:

- Divergent thinking and ability to perceive unusual and broad relationships

- Different time/space perspective

- Variety of valid alternatives from which to select careers

- Divergent modes of responses to problems

- Persistence of goals and a need to delve deeply into problems of interest

- Questioning, often critical, attitude.

In addition to the necessity of developing a program to allow these characteristics to benefit the learner, there is also the obligation to offer learning experiences that provide a challenge for gifted and talented individuals. Too often the materials and instruction are far below the capabilities of these students. Neither granting high grades nor commenting that the individual is not performing up to potential provides a solution. With respect to the individual who consistently performs at the top of the class

---

*Numbers in parentheses appearing in the text refer to the References at the end of each chapter.

without real challenge, James Gallagher draws an analogy to a talented high jumper who is required to jump at only two or three feet:

> He can soon get tired of such easy work and will certainly develop sloppy and poor habits that will ill serve him when he, in fact, is finally challenged. (4)

When gifted students sometimes fail to complete even the assignments that are far below their capabilities, the teacher may see the solution to this situation as enforcing the completion of the work assigned before granting any special accommodations for such students. The potential of these individuals will not be developed in this way, however, because the problem lies not with the required work but with the program itself. Since gifted students in many cases have already mastered the concepts and skills in the regular curriculum, they may see little value in going through the steps again. Consequently, they may not do all the work and as a result may receive average or poor grades. The loss is not only the effect of poor grades on future academic experiences, but more importantly the retardation of learning. Given a program that provides instruction commensurate with their learning styles, characteristics, and abilities, these individuals will reach far beyond the "regular" curriculum.

BENEFITS TO SCHOOL AND TEACHER

A special program for gifted and talented students often benefits the entire curriculum and atmosphere of a school, depending, of course, on the involvement and cooperation of the staff throughout the school. Individual teachers who see such a program as a positive step tend to relay this attitude to their students who, in turn, may also take pride in the program, even if they are not directly involved in it. Usually, however, most students are unconcerned about academic programs and see everything in the school system, except lunch and athletics, as "just education." The enthusiasm and attitudes of those in the gifted and talented program may permeate a school if students are allowed to share their enthusiasm and interests. This atmosphere can help counteract the anti-academic tone that pervades many of our educational institutions.

Although many teachers envision the removal of students with exceptional ability as a loss to the overall instruction of the class, the reverse may be true for the following reasons:

1. This separation lessens the range of intellectual and reading abilities with which the teacher has to contend. In most classes the abilities range from 70 to 140 in IQ with an even wider gap—perhaps as many as eight levels—between the poorest and the best readers. In an effort to provide instruction at all levels, many teachers group students, provide individualized instructional programs, or teach to the average and try to tutor those who fall behind. With a smaller range, the teacher can devote more time and effort to various groups within the class.

2. The presence of these extremely able pupils is often frustrating as teachers find they are unable to provide sufficient motivation and flexibility for them to pursue their interests in depth. Since much of the teacher's time is devoted to instruction of basic skills at the elementary and middle school levels and knowledge of content at the high school level, little opportunity exists for work with those students who are far beyond such instruction. In addition, few teachers at the elementary level have the depth of knowledge in different content areas to provide gifted learners with adequate resources. These situations can be a continual frustration to the conscientious teacher who feels the need to provide legitimate educational experiences for all. A program that provides opportunities for the gifted to develop their potential can alleviate this source of teacher frustration.

3. Sometimes when the gifted students are separated, other students begin to play a more active role in the classroom. Having relied on the gifted for responses, these other learners now find they have to provide the greater part of class participation. They may also develop more confidence in their own abilities as they begin to assume new roles in the classroom vacated by their gifted peers.

BENEFITS TO SOCIETY

Although it may be difficult for some to imagine a young student as an adult, it should be kept in mind that the gifted and

13

talented individuals currently going through our educational institutions are the probable leaders of our society in the near future. Indeed, as has frequently been stated, these young people are our country's greatest resource for they are the ones who will shape our institutions, values, and cultures. We educators, then, should provide positive vehicles to help them assume productive leadership to benefit themselves and society to the maximum of their potential. Too often, however, their progress is impeded when they are forced to maintain the same rate and follow the same route as everyone else progressing slowly through the academic hierarchy. Furthermore, in our society most of those who assume leadership roles follow professional tracks, forestalling their entrance into a socially productive stage until the late twenties or early thirties, having continued their studies through advanced academic and professional degrees. To permit these individuals to be of maximum service to society, educational programs are needed that allow them to enter productive stages earlier and that encourage meaningful productivity throughout the educational process.

In addition to helping gifted and talented individuals achieve productive stages, we should also endeavor to provide experiences that will help them acquire vital skills, concepts, self-awareness, and social understandings. Eliot Wigginton, President of Foxfire Fund, Inc., an educational organization in Georgia that advocates student-initiated learning and community-based education, reflects on the role of the teacher:

> The products and the activities are real, believing as we [at Foxfire] do that the best way to teach and hone the skills we want our students to have (whether grammatical or mathematical or physical or analytical or legal or creative) is by plunging them into real work that requires those skills.... If it were put into the form of a directive that all our staff members were to follow, it would go something like this: Before you start to do anything related to your work with this organization, ask yourself first why a student is not doing it instead. If you don't have a good reason, then go and find a student—preferably one who has never done it before.... That's not the lazy way out. In fact, it's the harder way out. The job often takes longer. Mistakes are made. That, of course, is why an adult in most organizations usually does the job instead. Rule: An adult who habitually says, "This is a job that must be done, and must be done correctly and well, and therefore I must do it myself," must never be allowed to be a teacher. The only things left in his world for students to do are menial, meaningless tasks and exercises that have

14

no real bearing or real consequence in the real world. A school full of teachers like that does not graduate competent, responsible, self-confident, sensitive seniors. Ever. Except despite that school. Rule: We have to have more confidence in our students than they have in themselves. (18)

Throughout most curricula, emphasis is on acquisition of skills and knowledge. At the higher levels of learning, problem-solving techniques are stressed so that individuals will be able to cope with situations that may confront them outside school. For potential leaders, however, this approach is not sufficient. We do not want individuals who can just solve everyday problems; rather we need those who have the ability to perceive potential problems before they become insurmountable. We need problem finders. As Gallagher points out:

> The computer world that lies just over the horizon can easily handle the memory and problem-solving aspects of our problems, but the computers cannot, as yet, choose which problems are important and need attacking. Problems such as population control, nuclear power, and poverty need to be seen far enough down the road so that the reactions to them are planned and not hastily improvised. (4)

MISCONCEPTIONS

Besides explaining the benefits of a special program for the gifted and talented, the developer should also be prepared to face the misconceptions and unstated fears that may threaten its implementation. Before the program may be effectively developed, several misconceptions and fears should be acknowledged and addressed. Otherwise they may arise at a later, more critical time and bring about the downfall of even the best designed program. Awareness of common misconceptions and concerns should help program developers anticipate potential difficulties and respond at the appropriate time.

When discussing the implementation of programs for gifted and talented students, it may be necessary to correct several erroneous beliefs people hold about these programs.

Misconception 1. The gifted are already provided for.

Critics of special programs often claim that too much money is spent on exceptions, that enough has already been done for the gifted or bright student. Many believe schools have already insti-

15

tuted programs for the gifted and that the real neglect is with the average learner.

The group that should and does receive the most attention is the "average." Nearly all teacher training concentrates on preparing the teacher to instruct the "typical" class of "average" students because this is the group most teachers have or will have in their classes. Most materials purchased for instruction are directed at "average" students because they constitute the bulk of the school population. Finally, most published curricular materials are designed for "average" students because this group encompasses the largest and most profitable market (17). Perhaps not enough is being done for the "average" pupil, but most resources are already being focused in that direction.

In 1972 the U.S. Office of Education concluded that the federal role in providing services to the gifted and talented was "all but nonexistent." The report found that twenty-one states did not provide any services for their gifted, and no state provided for a majority of its gifted. When elementary and secondary school principals were asked about programs for their gifted, 57.7 percent stated they did not have any gifted students in their schools. The reported concluded that at least three-fourths of the gifted population in the United States receives no special attention of any kind (2). According to Dorothy Sisk, former director of the U.S. Office of Gifted and Talented, the situation had not changed between 1972 and 1978. Even in 1978 only about 12 percent of the gifted individuals in our society were being served, and the federal allocation of funds for the gifted was minimal—approximately one dollar per gifted student (14). In summarizing the recommendations of the Council for Exceptional Children about education of the gifted, Zettel and Ballard state, "Most importantly, too many gifted and talented children are suffering from neglect that derives from the failure to provide the special educational support required to meet their unique learning needs" (19).

Misconception 2. The gifted will succeed anyway.

Although it is widely believed that special programs for the gifted and talented are unwarranted because these individuals will succeed on their own, the opposite is too often the case. Many gifted students do not succeed within the present academic setting;

16

they drop out of school or fail to continue their education beyond high school. After studying the dropout rate of the gifted in Iowa in 1962, Green found that 17.6 percent of these students in the state were not completing high school (6). A significant number of gifted students who remain in the system and who should be performing at the highest levels achieve only average or below average grades. In 1957, reporting his examination of the achievement of 251 gifted children. Miner concluded that 54.6 percent were working below levels of which they were intellectually capable, and that a majority of these students were working at least four grade levels below their potential (19). Mary Meeker, Director of the Structure of the Intellect Institute, found in one school that A students had IQs of between 130 and 136, but students with extremely high IQs had C averages (9).

These findings are not so surprising when we consider some of the personality and behavioral characteristics of gifted individuals—divergent and critical thinking and persistence in demands and questions. Many of these traits not only go unrewarded in classrooms but are often penalized as teachers sometimes regard them as unacceptable behaviors. This is borne out by the grades received by many gifted students and by the unreliability of teacher nomination of gifted students (7, 11). In their investigation of the gifted in regular elementary classroom situations, Gallagher and Crowder found that these children were poorly motivated and frustrated by the rigidity and intellectual sterility of the regular classroom (5).

While gifted and talented individuals often suffer in classes where no provisions have been made to accommodate their special abilities, they seem to succeed in special classes. In an extensive California study of 929 gifted students, grades 1–12, Simpson and Martinson found that those in special programs made significantly greater gains in academic achievement than those in regular classes. The gifted in special classes advanced an average of two academic years while the equally gifted in regular classes advanced only one academic year (13). Even a gain of two academic years, however, may fall below the capability of many individuals. In short, the gifted child may be able to maintain average growth if kept in a regular class, but the same child will probably not achieve full potential unless special provisions are made to accom-

17

modate and build upon his/her special characteristics. Indeed, without special provisions there may be regression. The lack of challenge and realistic goal-setting for the gifted may foster poor academic attitudes and lazy study habits that can further impede full academic achievement. The attitudes and habits instilled in the young become increasingly difficult to eradicate each year they are reinforced.

Misconception 3. The gifted student in a special program will have emotional and social problems.

Many people, including parents, teachers, and administrators, believe that the gifted and talented student will suffer severe problems with peers and self if set apart from age-mates. Most research has shown this belief to be false. Rather, emotional problems are usually brought on by the frustration of ability. In her report for the U.S. Office of Education, Ruth Martinson stated that researchers have found that gifted individuals who participated in special programs did not suffer social or personality problems, become conceited, or have additional health problems (8). Walter Barbe, after surveying graduates of Cleveland's Major Work Program, found that participation in special classes for the gifted helped a majority of these individuals adjust to different groups (1).

One cause of the misconception that gifted persons in special programs will have emotional and social problems is the story of William James Sidis, who entered Harvard College in 1909 at age eleven and died alone at age forty-six, having failed to achieve the heights portended by his giftedness. After researching this story and the lives of other gifted individuals, Kathleen Montour concluded that Sidis's tragedy was unique and that many other gifted persons who are allowed to proceed at their own rate and in accordance with their own goals lead successful and happy lives (10). Cecelia Solano, who also explored the relationship between precocity and subsequent achievement, concluded that gifted and successful adults can continue to demonstrate exceptional abilities and success, especially if their achievements are viewed in relation to their own goals (15).

Misconception 4. Special programs benefit only participants.

Perhaps the greatest stumbling block to the initiation of programs for gifted and talented is the belief that these programs will serve only the top three to five percent of the community and will not add anything to the education of the majority of children. Indeed, many believe that if the gifted and talented are separated, other students will suffer without their input.

First, in many situations where a program for gifted and talented exists, the total atmosphere and learning process throughout the school is improved.

The Delphi Program in Greece, New York, is a semiseparated program beginning in fourth grade. Students are homogeneously grouped for the academic studies and heterogeneously grouped for the rest of the day. A few of the Delphi students became interested in whales and began to investigate the problem in depth. As a result of their enthusiasm, interest, and continual sharing with everyone in the school, many students outside the Delphi Program have also taken a strong interest in the "save the whale" campaign. The interest has resulted in letter-writing campaigns, art projects, and extensive outside reading throughout the school.

Second, the removal of the gifted and talented individuals from regular classes does not necessarily detract from the total instruction for the other students. Actually, removing gifted children from a regular classroom may result in the stimulation of new leadership among students previously overshadowed. When some students know most of the answers and are highly verbal in their responses to questions, many other, less confident students may be reluctant to demonstrate their knowledge or they coast, relying on others to give the answers. By allowing the extremely able students to participate in their own programs, other students will have more opportunity to participate actively in the regular classes designed for their particular characteristics and learning needs.

Misconception 5. If gifted and talented individuals are selected for a special program, they will become elitist "snobs."

This situation does not usually occur because most students tend to regard such a program as just another vehicle for education. In a survey of student attitudes about inclusion in a special program

19

for gifted and talented, Barbara Ford found that most students (86 percent) felt they were not treated any differently by their peers after inclusion in the program than they were before (3). Sometimes gifted and talented students become less "elitist" when included in a special program because they find they do not have to be defensive about their abilities with their classmates.

Jack and Dorothy were considered "snobs" by most of their classmates and their teachers during their first few years of school. Not only did they know all the answers, but they continually lorded this knowledge over the other students. Finally they were placed in a homogeneously grouped program for the gifted and talented. Within a few months they abandoned their elitist behavior and began to interact naturally and equally with most of the other children in the school, including those not in the special program. Apparently, according to their teacher, the elitist attitude displayed in the regular classroom was a defensive posture adapted to overcome their feelings of difference from their classmates. When they were placed in a situation where they could interact with intellectual peers, they lost the need to display their superior abilities to the detriment of others.

In summary, our society has not provided sufficient funding or programs for gifted students, either in comparison with the average student or even with other areas of exceptionality. Research has demonstrated that the gifted and talented student does benefit from special programs, and some evidence demonstrates that gifted individuals are penalized when not provided with special attention. In most cases, gifted individuals do not suffer socially, emotionally, or physically from placement in a program designed to help them achieve full potential. On the contrary, many educators believe that emotional problems will occur more readily if the gifted individual is not placed in a special program. Finally, a gifted program may help all students as it allows more pupils to participate and share in a wider variety of learning experiences.

Misconception 6: Something is better than nothing.

Too often people assume that as long as schools create something for the gifted, they have fulfilled an obligation and satisfied the needs of these students. Many of these programs, however, have been implemented primarily because they calm the parental outcry and are administratively simple. Several of the "pullout" programs fall within this category. In this model students receive differentiated instruction only during their part-time special class. Time spent in these pullout classes varies from less than an hour to a full day per week. This approach poses a variety of difficulties and concerns:

- Instruction for the gifted student is fragmented and nonsequential.
- Activities in the "gifted" class have little or no relation to activities in the regular class.
- Gifted students receive instruction commensurate with their characteristics only during the "pullout" time.
- Teachers of the "regular" classes tend to assume the needs of the gifted are satisfied by the pullout program and, consequently, may not make any additional provisions for them.
- Instruction for the gifted is isolated from "real" learning in the basic areas of English, mathematics, social studies, science, and reading, except as tangential special activities.
- Regular classroom teachers often feel the pullout program interferes with the instructional routine; therefore, they resent the student's absence from class to attend that program.
- Because underachieving gifted students are usually not selected for pullout programs, they have little opportunity to learn in accordance with their characteristics and abilities.

As Cox, Daniel, and Boston state, perhaps the most

serious drawback (of the pullout program) is the false sense of accomplishment it can provide a district; it is easy to establish such a program and believe the needs of able learners are being met. But at best they are being met only part of the time. Moreover, the pullout is not an easy first step that leads to more comprehensive programming. (F, p. 44)

If the pullout program is all a school will offer without some infusion in the regular class, something may not be better than nothing. If a school has nothing, at least the school and community may still be open to more comprehensive programs to address the needs of the gifted.

UNSPOKEN CONCERNS

The preceding misconceptions present problems, but they may be overcome with direct replies. A more difficult resistance arises from those concerns and fears that remain unspoken. While the concerns exist, direct replies are difficult as few individuals will acknowledge them.

Unspoken Concern 1. We are averse to helping others become superior.

Our system is based on the principle that everyone is equal. Although this means that all people should have equal opportunities to achieve their potentials, it is often interpreted as everyone being the same. In his short story "Harrison Bergeron," Kurt Vonnegut illustrates the danger of this trend when taken to an extreme, as those with above-average abilities are forced to remain average through physical encumbrances imposed by the "Handicapper General," Diana Moonglompers. While few would suggest going so far to maintain equality, some people are reluctant to allow individuals to move beyond the average in school. For example:

When Bill entered school, he was excited about the prospects because he had been reading for two years and he could compute simple arithmetic in his head. His excitement was turned to anxiety as he soon learned that he would not be able to read in school for another year because reading was not taught until first grade. Even then he would be held back since he was reading books at the fourth grade level that he could not get until he was in fourth grade.

As Gallagher remarks:

To many people, there is something manifestly unfair about giving Cranshaw, a boy of superior opportunities and abilities, special help to do more with his superior abilities, when other children are still struggling to meet minimum requirements. To these people, it is disturbing that there is not a tidy balance sheet for life. (4)

Unspoken Concern 2. The individual with superior intellect will turn against humankind.

This apparently absurd statement has been perpetuated through several media, including novels, film, and comics, for many years. Frequently the villain in these dramatizations is either a twisted scientist bent on destroying the world for some pseudoscientific

22

goal, such as bringing the dead back to life, or an evil genius striving to dominate the world. The hero, on the other hand, is usually an individual of average intelligence who because of superior strength and luck is able to overcome the villain and save humankind. Even historical accounts tend to emphasize geniuses who caused destruction above those who produced beauty. More of us are aware of Adolf Hitler and his exploits than of Albert Schweitzer and his deeds. The former is more dramatic and hence more exploited by the media than the latter. Consequently, this unconscious fear of superior intelligence is continually reinforced with few counterpoints.

Unspoken Concern 3. Gifted students will become independent thinkers and lose their respect for authority figures.

Although most teachers would hold the goal of educating students to be independent thinkers in very high regard, when it occurs many teachers and parents may block it. The student who continually challenges the teacher or the child who assumes too much responsibility too soon may encounter considerable difficulty in school and at home.

There may be a fear of loss of control over the curriculum if students are given opportunities to develop their own resources and program. Such loss of control presents two major problems for the teacher. First, without direct control over progress and rate, the teacher may not be able to cover all that is indicated in the curriculum guide and may therefore be in conflict with administrative forces. Second, many teachers enjoy their profession because of the opportunity to give information and knowledge to others. These teachers desire the student to be dependent on them as intellectual resources. As students become independent in their needs, the role of the teacher moves away from the authority figure and the dependent relationship is threatened.

Unspoken Concern 4. Gifted students pose a threat to established values.

Gallagher notes, "In essence, the inquiring gifted child is the true challenge to the educator and his own values, and the society and its values" (4). Many of the leaders of radical movements and peace demonstrations during the late 1960s and early 1970s were

23

gifted individuals following the dictates of the essence of democracy. In many cases, they were implementing rather than simply stating the principles upon which our society is based. Yet these individuals were also attacking many of the established institutions that had, in their view, violated these principles. Society did not readily accept them or their actions, although many of their demands have since been acknowledged as legitimate, albeit late. Gallagher writes:

> It is easy enough to say that we believe in the democratic process and the free exchange of ideas. If we do believe them, then we have the responsibility for allowing these youngsters the opportunity to explore answers other than only those which we think are correct. If we are honestly committed to helping them think for themselves, then we cannot impress upon them only our own concepts of what is right or what is wrong. (4)

The foregoing are a few of the misconceptions and concerns that may be encountered. In particular situations other questions, misconceptions, and unspoken concerns will exist. In addition, some people have such deep-seated feelings against special programs that they will not accept any answer to their questions. Although developers may not be able to anticipate all objections that might be raised, they can respond intelligently and forcefully if they have formulated a rationale focused specifically on their own situation.

References

1. Barbe, Walter. "Evaluation of Special Classes for Gifted Children." *Exceptional Children* 22 (November 1955): 60–62.
2. *Education of the Gifted and Talented: Report to the Congress of the United States by the U.S. Commissioner of Education.* U.S. Department of Health, Education and Welfare, Office of Education. Washington, D.C.: Government Printing Office, 1972.
3. Ford, Barbara. "Student Attitudes Toward Special Programming and Indentification." *Gifted Child Quarterly,* Winter 1978.
4. Gallagher, James J. *Teaching the Gifted Child.* Boston: Allyn and Bacon, 1975.
5. _____, and Crowder, Thora. "The Adjustment of Gifted Children in the Regular Classroom." *Exceptional Children* 23 (April 1957): 353–63.
6. Green, Donald A. "A Study of Talented High School Drop-Outs."

Vocational Guidance Quarterly 10 (Spring 1962): 171–72.

7. Jacobs, J. C. "Effectiveness of Teacher and Parent Identification of Gifted Children as a Function of School Levels." *Psychology in the Schools* 8 (1971): 140–42.

8. Martinson, Ruth A. "Research on the Gifted and Talented: Its Implications for Education." In *Education of the Gifted and Talented: Report to the Congress of the United States by the U.S. Commissioner of Education.* Washington, D.C.: Government Printing Office, 1972.

9. Meeker, Mary. "Differentiated Syndromes of Giftedness and Curriculum Planning: A Four-Year Follow-up." *Journal of Special Education* 2 (Winter 1968).

10. Montour, Kathleen. "William James Sidis, the Broken Twig." *American Psychologist* 32 (April 1977) 265–79.

11. Pegnato, Carl W., and Birch, Jack W. "Locating Gifted Children in Junior High Schools: A Comparison of Methods." *Exceptional Children* 25 (March 1959): 300–4.

12. Reynolds, M. C. "A Crisis in Evaluation." Exceptional Children 32 (May 1966): 585–92.

13. Simpson, Ray, and Martinson, Ruth. "Educational Programs for Gifted Pupils: A Report to the California Legislature." Sacramento: California State Department of Education, January 1961. ED 100 072.

14. Sisk, Dorothy. "New Directions in Gifted and Talented." North East X-Change Conference, New Haven, Conn., April 1978.

15. Solano, Cecelia H. "Precocity and Adult Failure: Shattering the Myth." Paper presented at the Annual Convention of the National Association for Gifted Children, Kansas City, Mo., October 1976. ED 137 667.

16. Vassar, William. *Conn-Cept.* Hartford, Conn.: State Education Department, 1976.

17. _____. "Policy Making for the Gifted." Unpublished speech. Board of Cooperative Educational Services, April 29, 1977.

18. Wigginton, Eliot. "Beyond Foxfire." *Walkabout,* March 1979.

19. Zettel, Jeffrey J., and Ballard, Joseph. "A Need for Increased Effort for the Gifted and Talented." *Exceptional Children* 44 (January 1978): 261–67.

Chapter 2
PROGRAM DESIGN

This chapter discusses the various organizational structures designed to meet the needs and to accommodate the characteristics of gifted and talented students. These structures may be divided into three general categories: totally separated, semiseparated, and integrated. Placement of a specific program within one of these three categories is determined by the amount of time the individual student spends with other gifted and talented students who have also been selected for the program. Following this discussion three approaches to programming for the gifted and talented are highlighted: *acceleration, enrichment,* and *counseling,* which may be embedded in other structures.

One of the basic assumptions underlying most of these organizational designs is that gifted and talented students should at some point be grouped together to provide for interaction and productive cooperation. While research in homogeneous grouping has been inconclusive, some studies have indicated that it is successful for the gifted, especially if provided across age groups and accompanied by special teacher training and preparation for the particular group. After reviewing research in this area, Ruth Martinson concluded:

> Those who oppose [homogeneous] grouping have relied on opinion rather than on evidence. Recent studies have shown that administrative arrangements (without curricular modification) for the gifted as such produce no change. Any plan must include active and appropriate intervention to succeed. (11)

Without materials, curricula, and instruction different from that found in most regular classes, the homogeneous grouping programs may be little more than administrative pipe dreams. In programs where these provisions have been made, some researchers have found that the gifted in homogeneously grouped situations fare better than they do in heterogeneous classes (18).

Other educators, however, question the practice of homogeneous grouping for gifted and talented. Halbert B. Robinson, for example, states, "The notion that mentally gifted children constitute a reasonably homogeneous group who possess a high level of general intelligence is a gross oversimplification" (17). These individuals differ greatly from each other not only in interests and personalities but also in areas of superior abilities. "Homogeneous" is actually a misnomer but is useful if all the limitations are realized. An individual may be identified as gifted and talented and effectively grouped to provide specific kinds of instruction and experiences geared for particular characteristics and abilities. Even this resultant group, however, is not "homogeneous" in the strict sense of the word as its members are not all the same. Rather, they constitute a group of students who have been selected from the general population on the basis of specified characteristics pertinent to a particular program. Within this group each member still maintains a wide range of diverse interests, attitudes, and areas of expertise that should be taken into account when designing curriculum. In short, gifted and talented individuals should be grouped in specific areas to provide for appropriate interaction and to focus on particular levels of skill development and content coverage, but this grouping should be flexible enough to allow for variation within it.

A second basic consideration in developing a program for students is that of differentiation. How will this program differ from those programs already in place? If there is little difference, then the program may not be worth the time, effort, and money required to put it in place. The differentiation should be based on the special characteristics of the population for which the program is designed as well as on the goals of the program itself. This issue is addressed in greater detail on pages 102–5.

One factor that developers should take into account but sometimes overlook is the potential penalty to the student who participates in the program. This often encompasses two areas: time and requirements. If the program is conducted during periods of student participation in activities such as music, sports, or general recreation, students may be asked to sacrifice other interests in order to take part in the program. Sometimes developers have few options open to them about program placement, but if they are aware of potential conflicts for students, they may weigh these conflicts against any placement alternatives. A second penalty occurs when students are given a great deal of additional work or are graded on a higher scale than others. In both situations students are penalized for participating in the program by these commitments of extra time and effort. Usually some of these requirements are justified, but they should be kept in line with the goals of the program and the needs of individual students.

Keith, age eight, guards his free time ferociously so that he will have time to play, to watch television, and to read on his own. In making a decision about participating in a special program. Keith sometimes chooses not to do so because of conflict with his personal interests. Such a reaction may account for some frustration in teachers and administrators when an outstanding student does not participate in their program.

Consequently, when asking students to participate in a special program, we should realize the possibility that they are being asked to sacrifice time when they might be involved with other activities.

TOTALLY SEPARATED DESIGNS

Programs in which students are homogeneously grouped for *all* their instruction in a defined area of ability—academic subjects and visual and performing arts, for example—are defined as totally separate. In some situations students receive instruction as a separate group in all areas, including the specific one defined by program goals. Schools such as the City Honors School in Buffalo, New York, Hunter Elementary and High School and the Bronx School of Science in New York City, the Magnet School in Dallas and the Houston School for the Visual and Performing Arts in Texas, the Major Work Program in Cleveland, the Pineview School for the Gifted in Sarasota, Florida, and the Mentally Gifted Minors Program in California establish entrance criteria for students within their geographic region and gear instruction throughout the entire school to benefit the gifted and talented. In other totally separated designs, students are homogeneously grouped only for the specific area and heterogeneously grouped for all others, receiving separate instruction in the defined area and participating in other classes with the rest of the student body. For example, in the Delphi Program in Greece, New York, students are selected to participate in a self-contained class for their academic experiences, but they are integrated with the rest of the school for other activities. Also, the SMPY (Study of Mathematically Precocious Youth) Program at Johns Hopkins University provides special acceleration in mathematics while students may follow a regular curriculum in other areas; and the Governor's Honors Program in Georgia offers a career education and futures emphasis (20).

In other situations extended blocks of time, such as weekends or summer, are set aside for the program. The gifted in these programs receive specialized instruction only during those times and are usually integrated with other students during school hours. Perhaps the most firmly established weekend program is the Saturday Workshop of the Gifted Child Society of New Jersey. Summer programs also attempt to accommodate gifted and talented individuals as a group. The Governor's School in North Carolina, for example, selects students from throughout the state to participate in special summer experiences in various academic areas. Other summer programs such as those of Horizons Unlimited in Keene, New Hampshire, the Center for Creative Youth in Middletown, Connecticut, and the USDAN Program in New York emphasize creative and productive abilities. And the Gifted Student Institute in Arlington, Texas, conducts summer programs throughout the United States and Mexico. Such programs usually identify individuals in specific areas of giftedness and then provide instruction to help them achieve their potential in these areas.

SEMISEPARATED DESIGNS

Students in these programs receive instruction in both heterogeneous and homogeneous groupings. In many instances they participate in regular classes for most of their instruction, but they are encouraged to devote some time—a free period, after school, or part of a day once a week—to additional experiences within a particular area of instruction. Throughout the rest of the time they receive instruction in that area in the regular classes. In some of these situations students are "pulled out" of their classes or released from school for short periods during the week for supplementary or extra instruction. These special classes may be handled in several ways: by itinerant teachers trained to work with gifted and talented, by mentors, or by other individuals with expertise in a particular area. In any such situations the developer should strive to maintain close communication between the teacher of the special class and the teacher of the regular class; otherwise, severe problems may arise. First, unless the special teacher and the regular classroom teacher interact and communicate effectively, the student may be penalized for participating in the program by being given extra work requirements to "make up" work missed in class. Second, some classroom teachers may feel threatened by having "experts" take children out of the class for special programs and their attitudes toward the program may be communicated to the students involved. Third, untrained teachers of the special class, such as mentors, may not fully understand the purpose of the program or the characteristics of the students and may consequently fail to provide an appropriate experience for them. The interaction between the special teacher and the classroom teacher should help each one provide appropriate instruction for the gifted and talented individuals in the program as they share information about materials, curriculum content, and approaches. It should also help to avoid duplication of effort, to allow students to demonstrate their abilities, and to increase their learnings effectively.

INTEGRATED DESIGNS

Some schools attempt to accommodate the gifted and talented without modifying the general structure. Instead, the classroom teacher provides individualized instructional programs and packets and special projects. To provide a productive learning experience for the gifted, these approaches often require a wide range of expertise in many areas, vast resources, and teaching techniques that many teachers feel they do not have. In these programs the classroom teacher may have to work with physically handicapped, emotionally disturbed, learning disabled, gifted and talented, as well as with the majority of students who fall within the range labeled "average." In such circumstances one or more groups may fail to receive the necessary attention and appropriate instruction. When a decision must be made about where to focus time and

30

effort, the gifted and talented may be overlooked or given more of the same inappropriate work to keep them occupied.

On the other hand, some teachers have been able to develop expertise and techniques to work effectively with gifted in the regular class. The development of expertise has required extra training in identifying and working with gifted and talented and help with designing appropriate individualized learning programs. These programs, however, must be more than packets and solitary experiences because all students need the opportunity to interact with others of similar interests and abilities. (See Selected References, Gartner and Riessman.)

ACCELERATED PROGRAMS

One of the more controversial approaches to education for the gifted and talented is the accelerated program. These programs may take different forms, including early admission to kindergarten, high school, and college; rapid movement through grades; and the bypassing of grades in specific subject areas. Critics suggest that acceleration is not appropriate because the individual will not be able to interact socially and emotionally with chronological peers.

Other educators, however, have indicated that acceleration not only helps the gifted and talented, but that failure to accelerate may harm the individual. While citing the advantages of acceleration, Bish notes that emotional problems may result from keeping gifted students in classes that do not challenge them, and that acceleration tends to contribute to increased social maturity in gifted students (2). After surveying the research, Stanley states that acceleration through college will not hurt the emotional development of the gifted individual. He concludes that nonacceleration often frustrates the learning pace of gifted students and results in emotional and academic problems (19).

Gold, after reviewing the research, concludes that when standards for acceleration are maintained, the accelerated individuals will probably reach higher levels of academic achievement and will not suffer more emotional problems than nonaccelerated students. He cautions, however, that acceleration should not exceed two years throughout the twelve-year program (5). Gold also cautions

31

against more acceleration without modification of the curriculum to meet the gifted individual's unique abilities (4). Renzulli, too, warns against acceleration without modification, as instruction would probably not be geared to gifted individuals but rather to older students in a regular class. "Then everyone ends up marching to the tune of the same drummer, albeit at a faster rate" (16).

In sum, acceleration can benefit the gifted individual, especially if care is taken with the selection and the program. It seems most advantageous to initiate acceleration early, selecting those gifted children who display social maturity as well as intellectual superiority. Finally, the accelerated program should provide more than just rapid movement through the grades. The curriculum should be modified to build upon the particular learning characteristics of the gifted and talented individuals involved in the program.

ENRICHMENT PROGRAMS

These programs usually involve supplementing the regular curriculum with activities that provide more opportunity to explore in depth the topic or area of study. The varieties of enrichment are limited only by the imagination, including independent study, supplemental learning kits or packets, field trips, and mentors, or full classes with extended opportunities.

Successful enrichment programs for gifted students usually require the student to move beyond the routine acquisition of knowledge to examine relationships among different areas or to delve deeply into a few areas. The less effective programs fail to differentiate among students and require the gifted to do the same as everybody else, only faster and more often. These programs do not take into account characteristics of the gifted such as their ability to draw abstract generalizations; to pursue topics of interest in great depth; to analyze, synthesize, and evaluate with little guidance; and to communicate ideas well in a variety of ways.

Another problem with some enrichment programs for the gifted is that they may stop far below the levels of the students. While these programs may provide a variety of activities, too often they do so without sequence, direction, or ultimate goals, being merely a patchwork of good intentions. As T. Ernest Newland suggests: "The numerous, and soon monotonous, things which bright children can do as teacher aides, the number puzzles which may be solved, the wide variety of charts ... to be constructed and maintained, and the like, are but intellectual atoms which too often are more a gesture of a shallow educational diversion than of true enrichment" (13). Successful enrichment programs for the gifted and talented build upon their characteristics and challenge them to explore new areas of thinking and responding. Such programs should provide a sequence of experiences designed to promote continuous fulfillment of the potential of gifted students.

The mentor type of enrichment program has offered valuable learning experiences, but mentors must be carefully selected to challenge the learner sufficiently. Bruce Boston suggests that in programs that stress interaction between gifted students and mentors, emphasis should be on observation, perception, and problem finding and problem solving, rather than on verbal dissemination of information to the gifted individual. Boston also recommends that both the gifted student and the mentor should be specifically selected for the program and should be carefully matched (3). Enrichment through mentor-pupil interaction may be especially valuable because it not only puts the gifted child in contact with a specialist in a given field, but it may involve the community in the program. Again, care must be taken with the pupil and mentor selection, and program developers must work with the pairs to be sure that the experiences fulfill the needs of the individual and the goals of the program. (See also Uhler [21].)

Other types of enrichment include accelerated subject matter units, team-teaching in specific areas, small group interaction, lectures and demonstrations, and instructional television programs (14). Although these techniques may provide valuable learning experiences for all students in a class, including the gifted, unless the focus is on continuous development of abilities, the experiences may fail to provide the gifted individual with sufficient challenge and sequence. They may be interesting and fun but not so fulfilling as they could be with appropriate development.

TWO RHODE ISLAND PROGRAMS

The Bristol Elementary Schools use a semiseparated design with all identified students attending a special three-hour class each

33

week. While the teacher has delineated specific skills to be developed during these sessions, the students' primary work consists of extensive individual or small-group projects. Before and during the work on the projects, students also receive instruction in advanced critical thinking and problem-solving skills.

In the Warwick Public Schools we designed a pullout program (grades 2–5) for twenty elementary schools with three teachers. The program entails a unit approach, combining large- and small-group instructional sessions and guided individual work. Large-group sessions are conducted at a central resource center by the program teachers every other week for a two-hour period. On alternate weeks students meet in small groups in their own schools for a forty-five-minute session conducted by a program or classroom teacher. In addition, students are given at least one hour each week during school hours for individual study. The program teachers help the classroom teachers compress instruction for the participants to give them time in class to make up vital work missed and to complete program tasks. This also facilitates communication between program and classroom teachers.

COUNSELING

A vital but often neglected component of programs for the gifted and talented focuses on their emotions and attitudes, their affective needs. While important for all students, counseling and guidance for the gifted should incorporate areas unique to their specific characteristics (see *Characteristics and Identification of Gifted and Talented Students*) as well as general areas of guidance. For example, because the mental ages of gifted children exceed their chronological ages, they are often expected to be more emotionally mature than their age-mates. "In fact, it is more likely that they will be somewhat more mature than chronological expectations, but closer to [chronological age] than to mental age" (6).

Because the gifted and talented may be more mature than their chronological peers, they may be treated as adults when they are, indeed, still children. Such treatment and resultant expectations may create emotional difficulties not encounterd by other children. Teachers, parents, and even counselors may fail to recognize these and other special needs of the gifted and talented.

Some particular areas of counseling needs for the gifted result from their special characteristics. First, many gifted individuals have difficulty selecting one area upon which to focus for future studies or vocation. While most of us have a limited choice since we can excel in only a few areas, some gifted individuals possess superior abilities and intense interests in many areas. This is advantageous on the one hand but anxiety-producing on the other, for the gifted individual may face conflicting pressures to choose various avenues. Some pressures lean toward those roads leading to monetary reward, others push toward those showing social conscience, and still others urge intellectual or artistic pursuits. Possession of these abilities and sensitivity to these pressures sometimes place individuals in situations where they avoid making a choice or a decision by just dropping out.

Other problems relate to peer relationships. The ability to understand concepts not envisioned by others may lead to a solitary position where the gifted child may be the brunt of others' frustrations. The resulting personal anxiety and frustration may cause complete withdrawal from the siutation, open rebellion against peers and teachers, or denial of the abilities and maintaining a very low profile in the situation. Without help, the gifted individual may not be able to cope with the problem and, consequently, may not develop those talented characteristics and abilities. Also, some gifted and talented individuals need help in interacting with others whose skills are not so advanced as theirs. They have to learn not only patience and understanding of others, but, perhaps more importantly, a realization that everyone has something to offer and that we should seek out each other's strengths, helping each other by sharing interests and abilities. Peer relationships, especially among adolescents, are very important for emotional security. Because of their differences from average students, the gifted sometimes need more help than most in establishing productive relationships.

Again, because of their advanced skills, many gifted students acquire personal fears of failure. As Gowan and Bruch observe: "Superior students often desire to excel, but this very need may be so great that they will not risk a mediocre or less than first-rate performance. Perfectionistic tendencies can limit activities which require new experiencing, or in which they feel unsure of

35

completing successfully" (6). This fear of failure may make it difficult for the gifted and talented individual to attempt any new solutions to problems or to try to solve problems that may be too difficult. To develop their abilities they need challenges and they should explore alternative approaches to problems. To do this, however, they may require help from parents, teachers, and counselors to acquire the security necessary for taking risks that may lead to failure rather than to success.

To help gifted and talented individuals develop emotionally as well as intellectually, teachers, counselors, and parents have to work cooperatively because all three groups are extremely important in this maturation process. Joseph Kandor of the State University of New York, College at Brockport, has suggested that this interaction may be facilitated by focusing on vocational choices using a decision-making model (9). For example:

1. *Identify a problem* Focus attention on specific aspects of difficulties encountered in selecting a career or on specific career choices.

2. *Identify alternative solutions.* Brainstorm many ways of overcoming the problem or many possible careers; list all alternatives without comment.

3. *Evaluate alternatives.* Explore positive and negative aspects of each alternative, including objective areas, such as future market, and subjective ones, such as self-gratification.

4. *Select the best alternative.* Realize that this selection applies only to present conditions and that if the conditions change, the selection may be modified. The choice is only the best at the time, not the right one forever.

5. *Try the alternative selected.*

6. *Recycle the selection.* Reassess the legitimacy of the selection by taking it through the procedure again. The first choice may not necessarily be the best.

This approach to problem solving and decision making may be used productively by teachers, counselors, and parents as they explore problems with the gifted and talented.

The Guidance Institute for Talented Students (GIFTS) at the

36

University of Wisconsin at Madison combines academic programs with guidance and counseling for the gifted. Philip Perrone describes the area stressed in the counseling component.

Diminish self-dissatisfaction.

Being different, even if it is being talented, frequently leads to negative feeling or self-dissatisfaction. It is most important to prevent dissatisfaction from occurring by helping build a positive self-concept from the beginning. Frequently talented students learn they are different from peers after the first year or two of school when they become sensitive to self in relation to others. When self-dissatisfaction occurs, the teacher should look for significant changes in behavior such as excessive withdrawal or aggressiveness.

Improve self-understanding.

Children need to understand their talents—and their accelerated development—in order to enhance their self-concept (or diminish self-dissatisfaction). Most importantly, each talented student should understand the intent or degree of accelerated development and whether it is general or specific (i.e., manifested in all or one or two aspects of scholastic performance).

Stimulate interests, initiative.

In part, the talented student should be given some freedom but particularly in elementary grades and to a lesser extent throughout school, teachers must provide much of the materials or structure many of the learning opportunities. The teacher of a gifted student could be compared to a coordinator.

Foster conceptual development.

Accelerated development requires appropriate learning tasks to help talented students continue their growth. Both conceptual (Piaget and Kohlberg) as well as metaphorical (Samples) development should be developed. Teachers may have to become more familiar with the literature regarding metaphorical development and divergent thinking.

Foster motivation.

When defined as an inner drive it is necessary to provide opportunities for motivated students to set their own course to a certain extent. However, motivated students will need help in structuring appropriate learning opportunities and they will need feedback regarding their performance. Faculty can also teach students how to evaluate their endeavors thus freeing them from being totally dependent on others for feedback and evaluation.

37

Foster an internal frame of reference.

Developing a value system, an internal locus of control and field-independence are related terms. In effect knowing and testing oneself, being motivated and capable of self-valuation is representative of someone with an internal frame of reference.

Achieve effective peer relations.

The talented student may require more teacher assistance with this task than all the others combined. Group dynamics in the classroom are the teacher's responsibility. Effectively orchestrating a classroom sitution with one or two pupils with accelerated development presents a challenge to any teacher. A beginning point is to have all students recognize and accept their somewhat unique levels of development similarly to how we accept (but maybe don't like) differences in height, weight, and speed afoot. (15)

Developers should carefully incorporate counseling into their overall program, stressing interaction among teachers, counselors, and parents. Although many assume that the gifted and talented have little need of it because of their superior abilities, some gifted individuals may actually have greater need of counseling than others. Gowan and Bruch cite two major reasons:

(1) The gifted arrive at an awareness of human problems, of values questions, and of their need to search for meaningfulness; (2) such students develop socially and emotionally over a longer period of their lives and to higher levels of social responsiveness and responsibility. Their early levels of awareness make them especially sensitive to the emotional reactions of others and to their own self-reactions. Their longer developmental range suggests they have a longer need for accessibility to supportive guidance. (6)

Case Study

Ralph's parents discovered that he could read fairly well when he was four. By his fifth birthday he was not only reading books from the Random House Beginning Reader's Club, but he was also doing addition, subtraction, and multiplication of large numbers in his head. He could write a little, tell time well, and make change as banker in Monopoly games, which he usually won. This information was not shared with the kindergarten teacher the following year.

One month after kindergarten started, a confrontation occurred between Ralph's parents and the kindergarten teacher. The child's behavior at home had deteriorated and he complained about getting into trouble in school for "talking." Apparently Ralph was reading the directions of his kindergarten workbooks and doing the exercises while the teacher was explaining the directions to the rest of the class. Although the teacher did not realize he could read, his classmates did. Therefore they often went to him for help with the exercises and he got into trouble for talking. After the parent-teacher conference, a first grade teacher offered to work with Ralph in her reading group. This meant that the five-year-old boy had to go by himself across the school to another wing, crossing through the gym during basketball games or walking around outside the school. In spite of the severe winter weather, Ralph pursued the outside route so that he could participate in the advanced reading group. Later, he was confronted with a more difficult decision when his kindergarten class changed from morning to afternoon session. Either the boy had to leave his friends in kindergarten or forsake the reading program. He chose to stay with his friends. During another parent-teacher conference, the kindergarten teacher told his parents that Ralph was doing well in arithmetic because he could count to ten. At home, however, he was using flash cards to do addition, subtraction, and division problems. The teacher did not give the child more advanced work because his penmanship needed improvement.

When Ralph entered first grade and scored 90 on a group IQ test, his first grade teacher realized he had more ability than was reflected by this score and had him take an individualized IQ test on which he scored 170. While this score demonstrated his superior abilities, Ralph could not receive help from the special education teacher or from a tutor because they were designated for the learning disabled. He was allowed to attend some science classes in the upper grades two periods each week for six weeks. The work there, however, was similar to that in his own class. During first grade he worked ahead in arithmetic, completing the first, second, third, and half of the fourth grade arithmetic books; and he read the most advanced second grade book for his class. His friends liked and respected him, and he enjoyed school.

In second grade Ralph was permitted to join the reading group with which he had worked when he was in kindergarten. The teacher of this third grade group held high expectations for the child and provided him with a great deal of extra work, often on projects of his own choosing. In other areas of the curriculum Ralph worked with his classmates at the second grade level, except in arithmetic in which he worked with an easy third grade text. Finding the drill in the arithmetic series repetitious, he constantly worked slowly in that book. His frustrations seemed to carry over to his peer relationships and his study habits. He began to get into fights during recess, and his friends drew away from him or made him the brunt of their jokes. While his work area at home was highly organized and neat, his desk in school was in constant disarray. His relationship with his second grade teacher was antagonistic on both sides. When his parents had the boy diagnosed by a psychologist, the psychologist reported that Ralph worked with speed and intensity, was overly concerned about failure, became frustrated when his answers were not accepted, and had a superior attitude toward others. He recommended no acceleration at that time. Ralph was, however, allowed to begin the fourth grade arithmetic book, which he had nearly completed the previous year.

When Ralph began third grade, his family was in the midst of a crisis with his father seriously ill. His new teacher told the child his reading was not up to her standards, but he was allowed to attend a fifth grade arithmetic class where his work was exceptional. Yet when he returned to his third grade class, he was teased by classmates for receiving "special help" in arithmetic. Finally, his frustration became overwhelming. No longer wanting to go to school, he seriously wondered what was wrong with him and began to talk about killing himself.

Outside school, however, Ralph won every honor available to a cub scout in his age range and worked on other projects for which he was too young to receive recognition. He also bowled and served as an altar boy. In short, the boy achieved recognition and satisfaction outside school and in the accelerated fifth grade arithmetic class, but he was continually frustrated in his third grade class. After a parent-teacher-principal conference, Ralph was allowed to move into a fifth grade program, leaving third grade and bypassing fourth grade completely.

The first two weeks of fifth grade were very difficult, both academically and emotionally. Having skipped fourth grade, Ralph had never had homework and had only begun to learn cursive writing. While the older children were impressed by his abilities on tests, they teased him about his writing and his inability to complete his homework. After considerable emotional stress and with support from home, Ralph began to master the routine of homework and the other organizational skills taught in fourth grade. By the third week he was playing basketball with his fifth grade classmates and seemed to enjoy school. Apparently his classmates are beginning to accept Ralph as a peer socially as well as academically. At age eight, however, he is now beginning to outdistance them in arithmetic and is ready for concepts usually reserved for high school. His parents are concerned about the next step.

References

1. Birch, Jack W. "Early School Admission for Mentally Advanced Children." *Exceptional Children* 21 (December 1954): 84–87.
2. Bish, Charles E. "What Are the Advantages and Disadvantages of Acceleration?" Administration Procedures and School Practices for the Academically Talented Student in the Secondary School. Washington, D.C.: National Education Association, 1960.
3. Boston, Bruce. "The Sorcerer's Apprentice: A Case Study in the Role of the Mentor." Reston, Va.: Council for Exceptional Children, 1976. ED 126 671.
4. "Educational Acceleration of Intellectually Talented Youths: Prolonged Discussion by a Varied Group of Professionals." Papers presented at the Annual Meeting of the American Educational Research Association, New York, April 1977. ED 142 088.
5. Gold, Milton J. *Education of the Intellectually Gifted.* Columbus, Ohio: Charles E. Merrill Publishing Co., 1965.
6. Gowan, John, and Bruch, Catherine. *The Academically Talented Student and Guidance.* Boston: Houghton Mifflin, 1971.
7. Havighurst, R. J. "Conditions Productive to Superior Children." *Teachers College Record* 62 (April 1961): 524–31.
8. Hobson, James R. "Mental Age as a Workable Criterion for School Admission." *Elementary School Journal* 48 (February 1948): 312–21.
9. Kandor, Joseph. "Counseling and the Gifted Student." Speech given at Greece Central School (New York), April 1979.
10. Keys, Noel. "Should We Accelerate the Bright?" *Exceptional Children* 8 (May 1942): 248–54.
11. Martinson, Ruth. "Research on the Gifted and Talented: Its Implications for Education." In *Education of the Gifted and Talented: Report to the Congress of the United States by the U.S. Commissioner of Education.* Washington, D.C.: Government Printing Office, 1972.
12. Morgan, Antonia Bell. "Critical Factors in the Academic Acceleration of Gifted Children, a Follow-Up Study." *Psychological Reports* 5 (March 1957): 71–77.
13. Newland, T. Ernest. *The Gifted in Socioeducational Perspective.* Englewood Cliffs, N.J.: Prentice-Hall, 1976.
14. Nolte, Jane. "Nearly ... Everything You've Always Wanted to Know About the Gifted and Talented." Wauwatosa, Wisconsin Council for the Gifted and Talented, 1976. ED 140 553.
15. Perrone, Philip A., et al. "Identification of Talented Students." Guidance Institute for Talented Students, University of Wisconsin-Madison, n.d.

16. Renzulli, Joseph. *The Enrichment Triad Model.* Mansfield Center, Conn.: Creative Learning Press, 1977.
17. Robinson, Halbert B. "Current Myths Concerning Gifted Children." Unpublished paper, n.d.
18. Simpson, Ray, and Martinson, Ruth. "Educational Programs for Gifted Pupils: A Report to the California Legislature." Sacramento: California State Department of Education, January 1961. ED 100 072.
19. Stanley, Julian C. "Educational Non-Acceleration: An International Tragedy." Address at the Second World Conference on Gifted and Talented Children, University Center, University of San Francisco, August 1977.
20. Torrance, E. Paul, and Ball, Orlow. "Which Gifted Students Apply What They Learn in Special Programs?" *G/C/T* 7 (March/April 1979).
21. Uhler, Sayer. "A Confederacy Against Gifted." *Phi Delta Kappan* 59, no. 4 (December 1977): 285–86.

Chapter 3
CURRICULAR MODELS

Several educators have developed models to help teachers analyze and develop curriculum for the gifted. Four sample models that teachers and program developers have found helpful—Bloom's "Taxonomy," Guilford's "Structure of the Intellect," Renzulli's "Enrichment Triad," and Tuttle's "Advanced Skills Curriculum"—are described here. Also included is a description of the Pyramid Project, a recently developed model. Since a thorough understanding of any of these models would require intensive study, the material provided will expose readers to the basic elements of each. For a more complete examination of the various models, the texts cited at the end of the chapter and in the Selected Resources for the Third Edition are suggested.

BLOOM'S TAXONOMY

In their effort to develop a system of analyzing classroom activities in relation to cognitive behaviors, Bloom, Krathwohl, et al. developed a taxonomy of educational objectives that has provided a foundation for curriculum development since 1956 (1). This practice has continued with programs for gifted and talented students with particular emphasis on the higher levels of cognitive behaviors. The six categories of the taxonomy represent a hierarchy of cognitive behaviors; each level incorporates all previous levels with the exception of evaluation, which may occur at any level.

1. *Knowledge.* This category generally reflects recall of information. Verbs often used to describe student behavior reflecting knowledge are *memorize, recall, state, identify, recognize, list, match, name.* A suggested activity in this category:

    List the main characters and their roles in *The Hobbit.*

2. *Comprehension.* In addition to the knowledge of ideas, this category incorporates those behaviors that demonstrate understanding of material. Verbs often used to describe student

behavior reflecting comprehension are *paraphrase, translate, restate, summarize, illustrate, interpret, explain.* A suggested activity in this category:

Summarize the conflict between Bilbo Baggins and Gollum in *The Hobbit.*

3. *Application.* As the title suggests, behaviors in this category demonstrate ability to apply understanding of concepts to other situations. For many students, especially the gifted, application may be a high-level behavior because a quality work will incorporate all other levels of the taxonomy. Verbs often used to describe student behavior reflecting application are *apply, produce, compute, solve, relate, use, construct, prepare.* A single suggested activity in this category:

Using the events described in *The Hobbit,* produce a map tracing Bilbo Baggins's adventure.

A more complex suggested activity in this category:

Relate Bilbo Baggins's ambivalent feelings toward his adventure of the ring to your own feelings about the first day of class in a new school.

4. *Analysis.* Behaviors in this category involve the ability to break down and describe the components of an item and the relationships of those components to each other and to the whole. Verbs often used to describe student behavior reflecting analysis are *analyze, discriminate, compare/contrast, distinguish, detail, classify.* A suggested activity in this category:

Compare and contrast the personality of Bilbo Baggins in *The Hobbit* with the personality of Frodo Baggins in *Fellowship of the Ring.*

5. *Synthesis.* This level of cognitive behavior requires ability to draw together ideas or materials from different sources to create something new. Verbs often used to describe student behavior reflecting synthesis are *produce, design, write, reorganize, create, generate, generalize.* A suggested activity in this category:

Using the settings and personalities of characters developed in *The Hobbit,* write a new adventure for Bilbo Baggins.

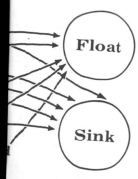

Float

Sink

cover categories and relationshi[...]
[...]theses (8, p. 81).

[...]OF THE INTELLECT MODE[...]

[...]of intelligence are closely associ[...]
[...]equently do not encompass all [...]
[...]ilford factor-analyzed intellig[...]
[...]ed the Structure of the Intel[...]
n Intelligence (2). This model [...]
[...]gence along three dimensions, [...]
[...]spects of intelligence at each p[...]
[...]d the model is a block with th[...]

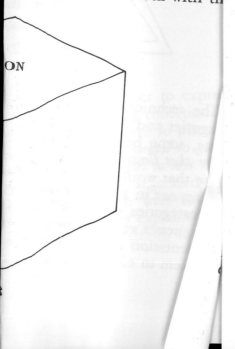

6. *Evaluation.* Behaviors in this category involve judgments about value, purpose, or quality of an idea or item. Verbs often used to described student behavior reflecting evaluation are *judge, criticize, assess, justify, appraise, rank, dispute.* A suggested activity in this category:

Justify or criticize Bilbo Baggins's taking the ring.

Although instruction ideally should involve all students at each level of the taxonomy, in practice most class time is spent on acquisition of knowledge and demonstration of comprehension. Many educators suggest that for the gifted and talented a greater proportion of instructional time should be devoted to the higher levels of analysis, synthesis, and evaluation. This approach for gifted students, however, does not omit work at the knowledge and comprehension levels. These students require basic skills and acquisition of knowledge and demonstration of comprehension in order to operate at the higher levels. On the other hand, they should not spend so much class time on these skills as other pupils do since most gifted students are able to acquire knowledge and comprehend information quickly and independently. The diagram on p. 47 illustrates the relative proportion of classroom emphasis on each level.

In addition to the cognitive domain, educators, especially Krathwohl et al., have also developed a taxonomy for the affective domain to describe emotional and attitudinal development (5). While these two domains are often cited as separate entities, there is constant interaction between them. In developing a curriculum, teachers must consider student attitude as well as intellect. Frank Williams has illustrated this with a component of his "Thinking-Feeling" model (8). (See also his *Total Creativity Program for Individualizing and Humanizing the Learning Process* [9].) Under pupil behaviors, he cites those shown in the table (8) on p. 46.

An activity exemplifying the interaction of intellect and attitude according to Williams's model might be the following:

TO ENCOURAGE: CURIOSITY AND COMPLEXITY
THROUGH: Arithmetic; Science
USING: Strategies No. 2—Attributes
　　　　　　　　No. 9—Skills of search
　　　　　　　　No. 14—Evaluate situations

Behavior	Meaning
COGNITIVE—INTELLECTIVE	
FLUENT THINKING To think of the most—	Generation of a quantity Flow of thought Number of relevant responses
FLEXIBLE THINKING To take different approaches—	Variety of kinds of ideas Ability to shift categories Detours in direction of thought
ORIGINAL THINKING To think in novel or unique ways—	Unusual responses Clever ideas Production away from the obvious
ELABORATIVE THINKING To add on to—	Embellish upon an idea Embroider upon a simple idea or sponse to make it more elegant Stretch or expand upon things ideas
AFFECTIVE—FEELING	
RISK TAKING To have courage to—	Expose oneself to failure or criticisms Take a guess Function under conditions devoid structure Defend own ideas
COMPLEXITY To be challenged to—	Seek many alternatives See gaps between how things and how they could be Bring order out of chaos Delve into intricate problems or ide
CURIOSITY To be willing to—	Be inquisitive and wonder Toy with an idea Be open to puzzling situations Ponder the mystery of things To follow a particular hunch just see what will happen
IMAGINATION To have the power to—	Visualize and build material images Dream about things that have ne happened Feel intuitively Reach beyond sensual or boundaries

Pin
Pencil
Paper
Button
Eraser
Pebble
Cork
Penny
String
Wooden Bea

This lesson helped children dis
well as to verify their own hyp

GUILFORD'S STRUCTURE

Realizing that most concepts
with intelligence tests and cons
intellectual activities, J. P. G
tests and activities and develo
model in *The Nature of Hum*
lineates various aspects of intelli
viding for isolation of different
of intersection. When illustrate
major dimensions.

OPERAT

PRODUCT

CONTENT

4

1. *Operation*—describes the major intellectual activities through which one processes information from the environment.
2. *Content*—describes the forms information may take while in the environment.
3. *Product*—describes the form information takes as it is being processed by the individual.

For each major dimension Guilford has then delineated several subcategories.

Operation, comprising the major intellectual activities or processes, has five subcategories:

Cognition. This requires recognition of information that may be conveyed in any form, e.g., dramatics, print, film, sound. A suggested activity in this category:

Show a child a picture of a common object that has a part missing and have the child identify the missing part.

Memory. This requires recall of information to which the individual has previously been exposed. A suggested activity in this category:

Display a tray of objects and have the child list the objects after the tray has been removed.

Divergent Production. This requires the generation of a variety of ideas from a stimulus. A suggested activity in this category:

Show a child a common object and have the child describe as many uses for the object as possible.

Convergent Production. This also requires the generation of information from a stimulus, but in this case the emphasis is on reaching a single, or conventionally accepted, result. A suggested activity in this category:

Play the game Twenty Questions, in which one player attempts to guess an item that another player imagines. The guesser can ask twenty questions to which the other player replies yes or no. If, after the twenty questions have been asked, the first player names the item correctly, he/she wins. Otherwise, the other player wins.

Evaluation. This requires making judgments according to an internal or external criterion. A suggested activity in this category:

Decide whether or not a particular fictional character's action was consistent with the personality developed by the author.

OPERATION*

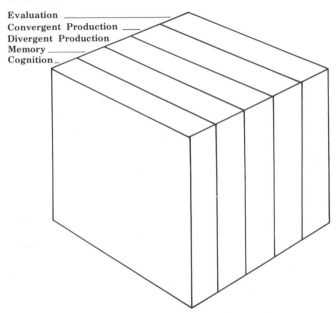

Evaluation
Convergent Production
Divergent Production
Memory
Cognition

Content, the broad classes or types of information an individual may perceive, encompasses four subcategories (6):

Figural. This information is perceived through the senses. It may be in the form of shapes, touch, or sounds. A drawing of a person or object, for example, is information transmitted through a figure.

Symbolic. This information is transmitted through a sign, something that is representative of the idea or feeling. A letter, a product logo, or a number, for example, is symbolic information.

*From *The Nature of Human Intelligence* by J. P. Guilford, Copyright © 1967 by McGraw-Hill Book Company. Adapted with permission of McGraw-Hill Book Company.

Semantic. This information is transmitted through spoken, written, or imagined words. An individual may have the concept but may be unable to verbalize it.

Behavioral. This category encompasses information transmitted through the nonverbal behaviors of others. "Body language," for example, would fall within this area.

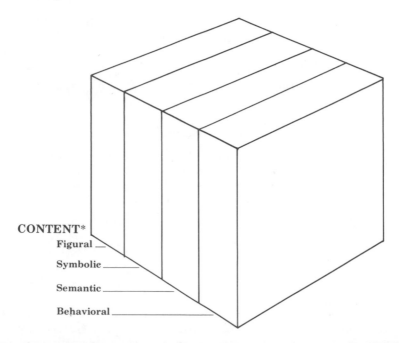

CONTENT*
Figural
Symbolic
Semantic
Behavioral

Product, the form that information takes as an individual processes it, has six subcategories:

Units. This type of information is processed singly. A unit can stand alone. The word "carrot," for example, is a semantic unit.

Classes. When units are grouped because they have one or more attributes in common, they form a class. "Vegetables," for example, is a semantic class.

---

*From *The Nature of Human Intelligence* by J. P. Guilford, Copyright © 1967 by McGraw-Hill Book Company. Adapted with permission of McGraw-Hill Book Company.

Relations. Those ideas or concepts that underlie the connections between units or make them a class are relations. In the following example the relation may be a statement such as "B is the natural class to which A belongs."

a	b	a	b	a	b
peach	fruit	pea	vegetable	beef	_____

Systems. More than two interconnected units form a system. The following example is a semantic system.

Solve the following problem:

> If you can buy two colas for 15 cents, how much would eight colas cost?

This problem system involves two quantities of colas (2 and 8) and two quantities of money. One of the latter is given and the other is to be found by the problem solver. He/she can solve the problem if (1) he/she grasps the combination of related pairs so that he/she knows what numerical operations must be performed, and (2) he/she performs the operations correctly (3).

Transformations. When information is changed or shifted in its function, it is semantic transformed. Puns, for example, are transformations. "A sign in a Texas restaurant reads, 'Remember the a la mode'."

Implications. These are expectations or predictions based on experience or previous information. Semantic implications, for example, often involve "What if ..." statements. "What would happen if all the electricity were turned off for a month?" Science fiction lends itself to implications and is often a favorite area with gifted students.

The intersection of the three components of intelligence forms a unit of intellectual ability or functions. If an individual recognizes a suggestive wink, she/he is performing the operation of cognition with behavioral content for a single unit. Also, where divergent production (operation), semantic (content), and classes (product) intersect, the intellectual activity would indicate divergent production of semantic classes. The following is an activity illustrating this interaction:

PRODUCT*

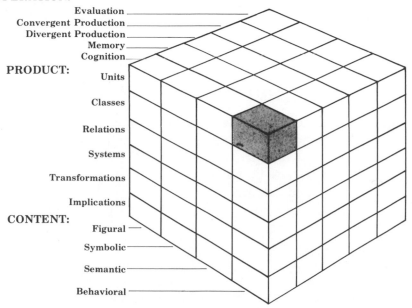

OPERATION:
- Evaluation
- Convergent Production
- Divergent Production
- Memory
- Cognition

PRODUCT:
- Units
- Classes
- Relations
- Systems
- Transformations
- Implications

CONTENT:
- Figural
- Symbolic
- Semantic
- Behavioral

Group the following words in as many different ways as you can: boy, toy, mother, boat, robin, alligator, and bottle.

The groupings are varied (divergent production), the words convey meaning (semantic), and the groups contain more than one word (classes). (See Activities for Teachers—"Curricular Models," pp. 152-56.)

The Structure of the Intellect model gives program developers a theoretical base to examine many aspects of intelligence not often included in most curricula because these areas are not identified by IQ tests. Some educators, such as Mary Meeker, have developed tests and activities derived from Guilford's Structure of the Intellect model.

For convergent production of figural systems a teacher might take a large map of the United States and cut out each state, making sure adjoining states are different colors. The student's task is to put the pieces back together to form the map of the United States. To accomplish this task the student has to select appropriate shapes of states and place them in correct positions in relation to the other states.

RENZULLI'S ENRICHMENT TRIAD MODEL

Joseph Renzulli of the University of Connecticut combined his research and experience with education of the gifted and talented to produce the Enrichment Triad Model (7) for curriculum development. This model is based on several assumptions about programs for gifted and talented. First, gifted students demonstrate certain characteristics such as persistence to a greater degree than other students. Second, enrichment should not be relegated only to programs for gifted and talented students; all students should have experience with higher-level thinking skills, problem-solving activities, and creative/productive thinking skills. Third, the highly motivated gifted and talented individual should have the opportunity to pursue real problems in depth and to present results of that pursuit to a real audience.

As the title implies, the Enrichment Triad curriculum consists of three types of enrichment that are not necessarily sequential. The first is Type I Enrichment, general exploration activities. The purpose of these activities is to motivate the student and "to bring the learner into touch with the kinds of topics or areas of study in which he or she may have a sincere 'interest' " (7). Typical activities in this phase are interest centers, short discussions, films, and field trips. These experiences, however, should be the kind that could lead to more extensive research and involvement if the student wishes to pursue them.

Type II Enrichment consists of group training activities. The purpose of these activities is to teach specific skills, "to develop in the learner the processes or operations (the 'powers of mind') that enable him or her to deal more effectively with content" (7). Training experiences might, for example, involve problem-solving strategies, creative and productive thinking activities, as

54

well as specific focus on areas defined in Guilford's Structure of the Intellect model. Activities in Type II Enrichment are designed to develop specific abilities and may involve a variety of games, discussions, and experiences aimed at particular kinds of skill development. Experiences involving Type I and Type II Enrichment should be available to all students, not just the gifted and talented, as motivation, breadth of experience, and skill development in the areas mentioned are appropriate for all, not for just a selected few.

Type III Enrichment, individual and small group investigations of real problems, however, is designed primarily for the motivated gifted and talented students. As Renzulli states:

> Type III Enrichment differs from presented exercises in several important ways. First, the child takes an active part in formulation of both the problem and of the methods by which the problem will be attacked. Second, there is no routine method of solution or recognized correct answer although there may be appropriate investigative techniques upon which to draw and criteria by which a product can be judged. Third, the area of investigation is a sincere interest to an individual (or small group) rather than a teacher-determined topic or activity. And finally, the youngster engages in Type III activity with a producer's rather than consumer's attitude, and in so doing, takes the necessary steps to communicate his or her results in a professionally appropriate manner. (7, p. 30)

At this time students move from learning about something to producing new products. They focus on a problem of real concern to them, treat it as a professional in that field would treat it, and finally present their product to an audience that a professional would consider appropriate. (See "Sample Primary Investigation" on pp. 121–22.)

Renzulli illustrates his model as follows, indicating that a student or group of students may move from Type I to Type III directly rather than progressing through a prescribed sequence (7, p. 14). (Note: See *Characteristics and Identification of Gifted and Talented Students*, 3d ed., for a description of Renzulli's "Revolving Door Identification Model.")

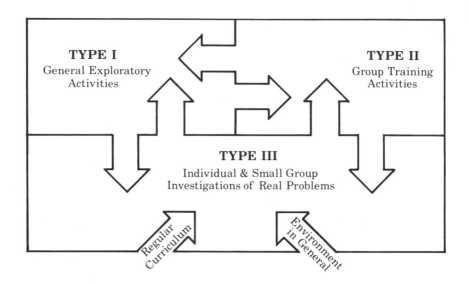

The Enrichment Triad Model*

TUTTLE'S ADVANCED SKILLS CURRICULUM

While Renzulli's Enrichment Triad Model was established for work outside the general curriculum, Tuttle's Advanced Skills Curriculum was designed for work in conjunction with the general curriculum. This model is based on five assumptions about the instructional process:

1. Gifted students should receive appropriate differentiated instruction based on their particular learning characteristics.
2. A curriculum should provide continuous development in specified skills and concepts.
3. Instruction should be cohesive rather than fragmented.
4. Instruction should enhance a student's ability to produce quality projects or works.
5. Interaction with others is vital to the learning process.

As in the traditional unit plan, the Advanced Skills Curriculum is composed of four phases: Introduction, Instruction, Culmina-

*Figure 1 (page 14) from *The Enrichment Triad Model* by Joseph Renzulli (Mansfield Center, Conn.: Creative Learning Press, 1977).

tion, and Evaluation, revolving around a single theme or topic of instruction. However, while the traditional unit plan separates the phases into distinct categories, in Tuttle's model there is considerable overlap of the first three phases with evaluation remaining a separate stage. The overlapping accomplishes two goals: (1) students are continually exposed to motivating experiences even during the instruction phase, and (2) students begin their culminating projects early, while they still have time to acquire more information and skills and to revise appropriately.

The emphasis on instruction in specific skills and concepts during the instructional phase provides continuity and sequence throughout the program, an important criterion in any effective program. Within the instructional phase the teacher provides direct instruction in general skills such as critical thinking and problem solving and/or advanced content skills and concepts. Throughout the instruction and culmination phases students should receive periodic reaction to their work from both peers and teacher. Consequently, final evaluation is conducted separately, since by this phase the student product should be complete.

The overlap and purpose of the respective phases are shown in the outline on p. 58.

The Advanced Skills Model may be implemented in either a homogeneous or a heterogeneous situation. The first illustration that follows exemplifies implementation in a self-contained middle school cluster of selected students; the second exemplifies implementation in a heterogeneous class.

Sample Implementation in Two Classes

In the A.I.P. (Advancement of Individual Potential) classes (grades 5-7) in Boston Public Schools, District III, students worked with the content of the general curriculum while developing critical thinking skills through work at the higher levels of Bloom's Taxonomy. This instruction was sequenced for each content area across grades 5, 6, and 7. The following activity illustrates student work in the English class on character analysis and comparison/ contrast of character and culture. First, students brainstormed a list of contemporary heroes. After compiling the list, they selected one or two major figures and brainstormed their heroic characteristics and deeds. Then they discussed the relationship between the

57

Advanced Skills Curriculum*

Phase	Purpose
Introduction	Motivate and interest students. Introduce new concepts. Provide ongoing interest activities.
Instruction	Provide direct instruction in advanced skills as well as a reinforcement of other skills. Provide instruction in content.
Culmination	Provide opportunities for students to work independently or in small groups to produce quality projects or works demonstrating implementation of advanced skills.
Evaluation	Assess the ability of students to implement the advanced skills in quality projects or works. Assess the effectiveness of instructional activities.

*Frederick B. Tuttle, Jr., 1981 (P).

deeds and characteristics and the values of the culture the heroes represented. This activity was repeated with heroes from myths previously read and analyzed. After comparing the heroes in all three areas (characteristics, deeds, and cultural values), the students discussed the differences and similarities. Finally, they drew conclusions about what makes a hero and how this concept has or has not changed over the centuries.

Some schools elected to maintain a heterogeneous class structure, therefore a small group of identified students was placed in each of three general classes. While the class was studying Greek mythology, the identified students used the same basic content to develop advanced skills in comparison/contrast and drawing conclusions. After the whole class read and discussed an introductory Greek myth focusing on the elements of mythology as related to character, plot, setting, and theme, the identified students began to work on their own, using specially designed worksheets as guidelines. They read several Norse myths and compared their characteristics with those of the Greek culture. They then drew some conclusions about the relationships between the mythology of the two cultures and between mythology and culture in general, and presented their results to the rest of the class. The identified students did not read more myths than the other students. Rather, they read different myths, applied a higher level of analysis to them, and synthesized information from several sources to arrive at more complex conclusions than the rest of the class.

Skills Activities in Content Areas

The following are some additional activities that could be used to develop advanced skills at appropriate grade levels within the theme of "Futures."

- *Reading and Language Arts:* Students could read science fiction and articles about the future. In addition to gathering information from printed materials, they should also obtain ideas from films, television, and radio. On the basis of information from these sources, students could describe aspects of the society of the future, e.g., eating habits, typical days in the life of _____, etc. Finally, they could pool their ideas and write short stories or scripts based on their discussions.

59

- *Social Studies:* Students could read articles or watch documentaries to obtain information about current trends. In addition, they could also interview leaders within the community who might be aware of the trends within specific areas such as economics, employment, education, or politics. Finally, students should pool their information and ideas, attempting to predict what may happen in specific areas in the future; These predictions should be based on past and present trends in the various areas.

- *Math:* Using information obtained from reading, viewing, and interviewing, students could develop graphs and charts illustrating trends in various areas. They could also conduct probability experiments so they can become adept at making predictions based on numerical data.

- *Science:* Students could explore several areas such as resource depletion, scientific progress, and medical advances in particular fields and form hypotheses about what will happen in the various areas in the future. They could also conduct experiments such as those involved in alternative energy sources to study future applications.

Culminating Projects

During the latter part of the instructional phase, students following the Advanced Skills Model would begin to apply their learnings to projects. The following are some possibilities:

- Write stories about life in the future.

- Develop a "futures" newspaper depicting events and attitudes that may logically arise in the future.

- Produce a dramatic presentation (radio, film, or television) depicting an aspect of the future.

- Write expository articles describing future trends and consequences of contemporary activities and attitudes (e.g., use of disposable containers).

- Design a city of the future, describing vocations, politics, homelife, transportation, energy sources, etc.

- Write articles exploring specific areas of contemporary life as they might evolve in the future (e.g., education, voting, use of computers in the home).

Possible Investigations

Purpose: To delve into a problem of personal interest for a real audience. Following are several problems that some students may wish to pursue, together with potential audiences. Have students generate other problems.

Problem	Audience
How can we make the community aware of "future"?	—Area convention for other students
Series of presentations, articles, magazines, comics, etc.	—Community—sell the magazine or newspaper
What community action can be taken about (environmental) problem that may be disastrous to community in the future?	—Presentations to local groups
Science Fiction: short story, novel, comic book	—Community—sell to students, submit for publication
"Futures" periodical (newspaper or magazine)	—Community—students in other schools (and own)
In-depth research and report	—Submit to journal

In order to help students follow appropriate problem-solving processes during their investigations, many teachers have found individual or small group contracts to be a valuable asset (see p. 62 for a sample contract).

Contract

Name:

General Area: Future Study

Specific Area: (e.g., science fiction comic strip)

Description: An ongoing comic strip with main character who (give characteristics). S/he lives in 2000. In this comic various current values and attitudes will be explored as they might be extended to the year 2000.

Intended Audience: Elementary and secondary students— readers of the "Futures Newsletter."

Dissemination: Publication of newspaper.

Procedure and Resources:

Steps: 1. Analyze science fiction for techniques of character development and extrapolation of trends.
2. Study cartooning techniques.
3. . . . .

Read: Lee, Stan, and Buscema, John. *How to Draw Comics the Marvel Way.* New York: Simon and Shuster, 1978
Asimov, Isaac. *Foundation.* New York: Avon Books, 1970.
Franks, Betty Barclay, and Howard, Mary Kay. *People, Law, and the Futures Perspective.* Washington, D.C.: National Education Association, 1979.

Submission Deadlines: Preliminary Proposal to Editor _____
First strip (draft 1) _____
First strip completed _____

Meetings with Teacher: _____
(date)   (purpose)

_____
(date)   (purpose)

_____
(date)   (purpose)

THE PYRAMID PROJECT

Still in the experimental stage, the Pyramid Project is an outgrowth of the extensive research into programs for gifted and talented students conducted by the Richardson Foundation (F). The major goal of the Pyramid Project design is to provide a comprehensive program to address the needs of the gifted in all content areas on a daily basis. The underlying premise is that students should advance as they master content. Beginning with enrichment in the regular classroom, students work at their own pace as they advance through special classes and in larger districts, into specialized or magnet schools. (See the diagram that follows [F]).

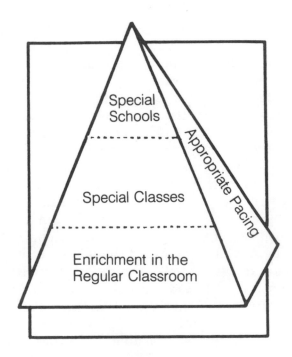

The Pyramid Concept

SOURCE: *Educating Able Learners: Programs and Promising Practices* by June Cox et al. (A national study conducted by the Sid Richardson Foundation.) Copyright © 1985 by the University of Texas Press.

The effectiveness of the Pyramid Project depends heavily on specialized training of teachers and the development of instructional materials and activities geared specifically for these students. As described by Kathleen Martin from Texas Christian University, the overall training program for teachers encompasses a graduate course, seminar, and field testing of activities and materials. Throughout the experience teachers engage in activities or investigations of problems that they might use with students and develop a variety of ways to solve the problem. Then they use this experience to create a learning module and instructional activities for students with the primary goal of leading students to raise questions and conduct investigations to answer their questions.

SUMMARY

These brief overviews of some theoretical models have been included to demonstrate the variety of resources that a developer may draw upon for background in curriculum planning. The model or general plan for the curriculum, however, should be kept in perspective with the characteristics of the specific learners and teachers. It is possible to become so involved with a model and with distinctions among terms that one loses sight of the classroom activity and the student. There should not, for example, be so much concern with the placement of a worthwhile activity under "analysis" or "synthesis" that it is omitted from the curriculum because its classification could not be identified. Rather, those activities that have proved valuable should be included even if they are difficult to categorize. In addition, activities may cross categories within a model, and it would be a mistake to alter an effective activity to force it into a predetermined mold. Such dissection of experiences diminishes their value and may hinder transference of the skill from the classroom to other aspects of the student's life.

Finally, when developing a curriculum or learning experience specifically for gifted students, teachers should strive to differentiate work for these students from that which would be appropriate for other students. As Sandra Kaplan states:

Curriculum for the gifted and talented can only be marked as such if it encompasses elements which distinguish it from being suitable for the education of *all* children. Curriculum for gifted students must be congruent with the characteristics that identify them as a distinct population. The answer to the question of why a student is gifted or talented is also the answer to the question of what type of curricular provisions should be developed for this child. (4)

Again, the ultimate focus of instruction is on the characteristics of the learner. (See Supplementary Materials, pp. 102-5, for examples of differentiation.)

A carefully planned program will include general approaches, comprising enrichment and acceleration as well as individual and group activities. The curriculum, regardless of model, should also incorporate work in both the affective and the cognitive domains. But in reality such a comprehensive and inclusive approach to programming seldom occurs without considerable time and effort.

References

1. Bloom, B. S., ed. *Taxonomy of Educational Objectives. Handbook 1: Cognitive Domain.* New York: David McKay, 1956.
2. Guilford, J. P. *The Nature of Human Intelligence.* New York: McGraw-Hill Book Co., 1967.
3. _____. *Way Beyond the IQ.* Buffalo: Creative Education Foundation, 1977.
4. Kaplan, Sandra N. *Providing Programs for Gifted and Talented.* Ventura, Calif.: Office of Ventura County Superintendent of Schools, 1974.
5. Krathwohl, D. R.; Bloom, B. S; and Masia, B. B. *Taxonomy of Educational Objectives. Handbook 2: Affective Domain.* New York: David McKay, 1964.
6. Meeker, Mary. *The Structure of Intellect: Its Interpretation and Uses.* Columbus, Ohio: Charles E. Merrill Publishing Co., 1969.
7. Renzulli, Joseph. *The Enrichment Triad Model.* Mansfield Center, Conn.: Creative Learning Press, 1977.
8. Williams, Frank E. *Classroom Ideas for Encouraging Thinking and Feeling.* Buffalo: D.O.K. Publishers, 1970.
9. _____. *A Total Creativity Program for Individualizing and Humanizing the Learning Process.* Englewood Cliffs, N.J.: Educational Technology Publications, 1972.

Chapter 4
TEACHER SELECTION

Thus far, students, program design, and curricular models have been discussed. A key element in the program remains, however: the teacher. Regardless of design and model, the ultimate impact on the student will be made by the teacher selected to modify and implement all other factors. Until recently only a few institutions have helped the teacher of the gifted. Although the number is increasing rapidly, still too few institutions of higher education have programs beyond a course or two for educating teachers of gifted and talented students. Most of the emphasis of these institutions has been on average students and on those with severe learning problems. As some of the problems of the gifted student become more evident, more courses and programs are being developed to meet this need. (See Supplementary Materials, pp. 107–9.)

Since schools cannot rely solely on course or program background to highlight potential teachers of gifted and talented, they must determine characteristics and attitudes that would help indicate these teachers. Several educators have compiled lists to do so. Such lists, however, are often based more on intuition than on research. Also, as Tannenbaum of Teachers College at Columbia University suggests, many effective teachers of the gifted do not possess characteristics found on these lists (1). A few teachers, for example, are able to work effectively with gifted students through some unknown tie that underlies the relationship even when the external characteristics seem to contradict this ability.

Project CITE-Gifted in Missouri (1978) conducted an extensive study to determine characteristics of teachers of gifted and talented and developed a competency-based program to help them develop appropriate characteristics and acquire necessary skills for working with gifted students. In reviewing the literature in the area, the CITE researchers arrived at several conclusions pertinent to teacher selection for the gifted and talented. In one area, they concluded that the classroom teacher does play an extremely important role in

66

the education of the gifted. Contrary to many popular opinions, many gifted cannot succeed on their own and need specially trained teachers in order to benefit more fully from their educational experience. The study also found that educators in the field stressed as important qualifications for teachers of the gifted and talented such characteristics as high intelligence, intellectual honesty, nonauthoritarian attitude, flexibility, curiosity, and psychological maturity (1).

After reviewing the research and literature on this topic, June Maker cited the following teacher characteristics as generally recommended: high intelligence, flexibility and creativity, self-confidence, variety of interests, sense of humor, sympathy with problems of the gifted, self-understanding, love of learning, and facilitator rather than director of learning. Of all these traits, she highlights three as most important: high intelligence, knowledge of subject matter, and emotional maturity (4). As Maker indicated, these characteristics would be highly desirable in any teacher, but they are vital in the teacher of the gifted. Since gifted and talented students tend to be persistent in their search for knowledge and especially perceptive of erroneous or superficial answers, the teacher of these students needs both the intellectual background to provide appropriate responses or direction and the emotional maturity to be able to cope with the superior ability and depth of interest of the students.

William Bishop explored the characteristics of teachers identified as especially successful by their gifted pupils. Many of his conclusions reinforce Maker's list: emotional maturity, preference for teaching the gifted, and intellectual superiority. He adds other characteristics, however: enthusiasm about the subject, pursuit of literary and cultural interests, businesslike classroom behavior, and preference for special educational provisions for gifted students (2).

Some researchers have reinforced the necessity of special training for teachers who plan to work with the gifted and talented. In addition to the learning of methodology appropriate for these students, special training is also necessary to change teacher attitudes toward the gifted. Cecelia Solano found that unless teachers have had some experience with gifted students, or courses in teaching the gifted, they would probably hold a stereotyped image of individuals in this group. This image is usually negative toward gifted boys and positive toward gifted girls (7).

Paul Plowman has suggested the following criteria for selecting teachers of the gifted and talented (6). Although the list was developed many years ago, the needs have changed very little.

1. Teachers of mentally gifted minors should be:
   1.1 Creative in
   1.11 thought   1.14 teaching methods
   1.12 production   1.15 materials
   1.13 classroom   1.16 experiences planned
        organization
   1.2 Well organized
   1.21 Deliberately advancing aspects of creativity and mental giftedness
   1.22 Using teaching methods, developing experiences, and employing methods of evaluation that are:
      (1) consistent with general and specific program goals and specific purposes, needs, and interests of individual children.
      (2) based upon a philosophy of education, principles of learning, a knowledge of social conditions, and awareness of relevant facets of personal, intellectual, and social development of each student.
   1.3 Enthusiastic—by example, instill a joy of learning, discovering, "self-starting," and sense of "mission" for personal growth and for improving society.
   1.4 Endowed with a sense of humor, empathy, and personal warmth that encourages gifted pupils to talk about, to think about, and reflect upon the things that are most important to them.
   1.5 Knowledgeable—Possessing broad knowledge, including superior knowledge in one field, an understanding of related fields, and insight into how knowledge from various fields may be applied in analyzing and in arriving at solutions to problems.
   1.6 Flexible
   1.61 In creating and restructuring the physical environment
   1.62 In using materials and equipment
   1.63 In structuring and restructuring interest—learning—personality—developing groups and classroom experiences
   1.64 In planning lessons and in modifying lessons to capitalize on a "moment of " or opportunity for learning.
   1.7 Aware of the capabilities and needs of gifted pupils.
   1.8 Resourceful in searching for and obtaining special materials, in becoming acquainted with and using resource persons, and in locating out-of-school places where children and youth may have worthwhile educational experiences.
   1.9 Providing special educational opportunities for each gifted pupil. (6)

Taking suggestions from several sources, a list of characteristics of effective teachers of gifted and talented students has been compiled. The selection of teachers for a program, however, should be geared to the specific area or areas of giftedness involved in the program.

The effective teacher of gifted and talented teachers is—

- highly intelligent
- flexible and creative
- self-confident and emotionally mature
- interested in many areas
- knowledgeable in subject area (especially at the secondary level)
- businesslike in classroom behavior
- in favor of special provisions for gifted students
- alert
- well trained to work with the gifted and talented
- extremely professional in attitude and actions
- intellectually honest
- nonauthoritarian
- enthusiastic
- intellectually independent

The traits cited are not unique to the teacher of the gifted. Indeed, most would be valuable characteristics for any teacher. Some traits, however, such as self-confidence and high intelligence, are particularly important in classes for the gifted because of the intellectual challenge presented by these students.

In addition to checklists, the selection procedure should also take into account classroom environment and the relationship between teacher and student.

We learn through experience and experiencing, and no one teaches us anything. but environments can.... If the environment permits it, anyone can learn what he chooses to learn; and if the individual permits it, the environment will teach him everything it has to teach.... It is highly possible that what is called talented behavior is simply a greater individual capacity for experiencing.

—Viola Spolin, quoted in
Reach, Touch, and Teach by Terry Borton (3)

If talented behavior is related to an individual's capacity to take in and process experiences from the environment, then a major part of the teacher's task is to create safe, stimulating, open environments that encourage exploration, sanction risk taking, and do not penalize failure. The CITE report highlights some of the professional skills a teacher of the gifted and talented should possess in order to create an appropriate learning environment. The CITE researchers found that these teachers should be able to create an atmosphere of inquiry and problem solving, to integrate ideas, and to unify affective and cognitive domains (1). Teachers of the gifted should also stress thinking and questioning activities, concentrating on exploration of ideas rather than coverage of content. Although they should have a working knowledge of a variety of curricular models (see Chapter 3), teachers should use such models cautiously. They should be able to integrate procedures to facilitate work with problems in a productive manner rather than create specific activities just to satisfy components of a model or taxonomy. In selecting teachers to work with gifted and talented students, administrators should seek those who can create an atmosphere that frees the learner to cultivate an openness to experience, a willingness to push the edges, to risk, to see new insights along old paths.

To create and maintain such an atmosphere, the teacher must be able to establish a productive and secure relationship with the class. As Henri Nouwen states:

> Our relationship with our students is first of all a relationship in which we offer ourselves to our searching students, to help them develop some clarity in the many impressions of their mind and heart and discover patterns of thoughts and feelings on which they can build their own life.... As teachers we have to encourage our students to reflection which leads to vision—theirs, not ours. (5, p. 63)

LOCATING THE TEACHER OF THE GIFTED AND TALENTED

Administrators or selection committees use a variety of approaches to locate teachers for programs for the gifted. Perhaps the most common approach is self-selection supported by professional evidence. Some of this evidence may include participation in conferences and workshops on educating the gifted, formal course work in that area, extensive readings about teaching the gifted, and classroom performance reflecting the goals of the program envisioned for these students. While interviews or résumés may demonstrate interests and efforts, it may, however, be necessary to look beyond these indications for other views of the individual's ability to work with the gifted and talented.

Other methods for locating appropriate teachers may involve peer nomination, classroom observation, and administrative choice. A behavior checklist designed for the specific program may help with each of these procedures (see the list on p. 69 and also Activities for Teachers—"Teacher Selection," pp. 156–59), as it would focus attention on abilities of particular relevance to the task. Such a checklist, in addition to the evidence just mentioned, would provide a more accurate indication of ability to teach the gifted and talented than arbitrary decision or seniority. Some general factors, however, such as general reputation or results of former students, should not be ignored. Certain teachers may not seem to perform the specific behaviors listed, but they do work well with gifted and talented students because of some underlying characteristics that may not be very obvious during a classroom observation or that may not appear on a behavioral checklist. Although the checklist may help to clarify some of the needs of the program and may serve as a valuable guideline for teacher selection, it should be used in perspective with other factors.

When a program for gifted and talented is envisioned, the search for appropriate teachers should be immediately initiated so that the teachers may participate in the development of the program. Since this search may not be possible because lack of information about the program, it may be more advantageous to involve several teachers in the development stage and to select from that group the classroom teacher for the program. This procedure has the additional benefit of involving several people in the development even though all may not participate actively in the program after implementation.

One school system enrolled all teachers and administrators who might work with the future program for gifted and talented in a series of workshops devoted to designing and developing the program. Not only did this procedure give all individuals with possibilities of involvement in the final program a voice in its development, it also gave all participants an opportunity to observe themselves and others working with the ideas, approaches, and materials supporting the program. Since the workshops were conducted as part of a college course, the participants also received graduate credit.

THE COORDINATOR

The coordinator of the gifted and talented program must possess multiple talents. An experimental background indicating adeptness at working with this unique population is critical. Equally important is an awareness and a pragmatic view of administrative policy and process that will facilitate the development and implementation of the program. It is advisable to target a person who possesses distinct skills in task orientation and human relations when seeking a candidate to fill this multidimensional role. While programmatic detail is paramount in the execution of a programming model, continuous articulation among parents, teachers, administrators, and students is of prime importance.

The person charged with the direction of the program has responsibility for making the decisions within the realm of the design. When this occurs, the coordinator is viewed as the prime facilitator in implementing administrative process and instructional design in the area of gifted and talented education. Once the coordinator has been appointed, his/her responsibilities should be articulated by the superintendent to staff and community.

References

1. Altman, Reuben; Faherty, Angela; and Patterson, John D. *Project CITE-Gifted*. Washington, D.C.: U.S. Office of Education, 1978.
2. Bishop, William E. "Successful Teachers of Gifted High School Students." Worthington, Ohio: State of Ohio Department of Education, n.d.
3. Borton, Terry. *Reach, Touch, and Teach: Student Concerns and Process Education*. New York: McGraw-Hill Book Co., 1970.
4. Maker, C. June. "Training Teachers for the Gifted and Talented: A Teacher Comparison of Models." Reston, Va.: Council for Excep-

tional Children, Information Services and Publications, 1975. ED 119 453.
5. Nouwen, Henri J. M. *Reaching Out.* New York: Doubleday and Co., 1975.
6. Plowman, Paul D. "Guidelines for Establishing and Evaluating Programs for Mentally Gifted Minors." Sacramento: California State Department of Education, 1962.
7. Solano, Cecelia H. "Teacher and Pupil: Stereotypes of Gifted Boys and Girls." Paper presented at the 84th Annual Conference of the American Psychological Association, Washington, D.C., September 1976. ED 137 667.

Chapter 5
PROGRAM EVALUATION

As with other components of program development and design, evaluation should be considered in light of the total product. The type of evaluation conducted, the evaluator, and the procedures used in the evaluation depend on the goals and curriculum as well as on the purpose of the evaluation. This chapter discusses the purposes of the program evaluation, the issues in evaluation of programs for gifted and talented students, and the concept of using a variety of approaches to program evaluation. At the end of the chapter a specific example of an evaluation is provided. For a more complete examination of this topic, see Renzulli's *Guidebook for Evaluating Programs for the Gifted and Talented* (2).

PURPOSE OF EVALUATION

There are several reasons for evaluating programs. First, a researcher may wish to determine the effectiveness of a given program as it exists without modification. Second, one may wish to describe a program to a specific audience, such as a school board, to justify requests for additional funds. Third, an evaluator may be interested both in the effectiveness of the program and in the ways in which it may be improved.

The purpose and type of evaluation will also affect selection of the program evaluator. Particular evaluators employ different techniques to fit the various purposes. The researcher, for example, would not modify the program while in progress, since it would affect many of the measures used on the problem situation and introduce unforeseen variables. The describer or fundseeker would probably not look for areas of difficulty, since they might reflect negatively on the effectiveness of the program and might endanger continuation of support. Ongoing improvement as well as final assessment are therefore recommended. In this way the evaluator makes suggestions for improvement throughout the procedure even though these suggestions may alter the structure of the program. Complete program evaluation should do more than just describe what is happening. As Reynolds points out, "The purpose of evaluation in education is simply to contribute to improvements in instruction, certainly not to justify projects" (3). Consequently the evaluator(s) of a program for gifted and talented should possess both knowledge of approaches and issues in educating gifted and talented students and knowledge of evaluation techniques.

Joseph Renzulli highlights the goals of program evaluation as follows: determining whether or not the objectives of a program are being fulfilled, discovering unplanned and unexpected results of the program, determining the effect of underlying policies and related activities on the program, providing continuous feedback about the program to participants, and suggesting both realistic and ideal program modifications (2). Prior to evaluation of the fulfillment of objectives, the program evaluator should examine the relationships among the objectives, program goals, identification procedures, curriculum, and unique characteristics of the gifted population selected for the program. All elements should reflect the special attributes of the gifted and talented students.

Some educators and researchers delineate program evaluation into two types: *formative* and *summative*. The main difference between the two lies in the purpose and timing of the evaluation. In general, *formative* evaluation focuses attention on improvement of a curriculum or program, while *summative* evaluation focuses on the effectiveness of a curriculum or program. Bloom, Hastings, and Madaus describe the two types as follows:

> Summative evaluation [indicates] the type of evaluation used at the end of a term, course, or program for purposes of grading, certification, evaluation of process, or research on the effectiveness of a curriculum, course of study or educational plan.... Formative evaluation is for the use of systematic evaluation in the process of curriculum construction, teaching, and learning for the purpose of improving any of these three processes. (1)

These types of evaluation, however, are not mutually exclusive. Both can perform necessary functions for the program and should be incorporated in the evaluation procedure. This would necessitate the involvement of *the program evaluator* throughout as the formative aspect occurs periodically while the program is in progress and the summative aspect is conducted at the end using data gathered periodically throughout the program. While the first type of evaluation helps to improve the program immediately by locating and aiding with specific problems that arise, the second type can give insights into the total program that may have been obscured by the daily routine or that may not have been evident through the use of the short-range instruments and procedures.

VARIETY OF APPROACHES

To examine the major dimensions of a program, educators should use a variety of evaluation procedures since different components of the program call for different techniques. For example, while growth in higher-level thinking skills may be evaluated through tests such as the Ross Test of Higher Cognitive Processes, these tests will not provide information about the quality of student projects; nor will they reflect classroom activity, nor student and parent attitude. Many developers in their desire for easily quantifiable information place a high priority on test results, leading them to an overemphasis on measurement of specific skill acquisition. This limited focus, however, will overlook important aspects of the program.

While some components of a program for gifted and talented may be evaluated through tests and analysis of student products, other areas, such as attitudes and opinions, may require the use of surveys and questionnaires. Some educators choose to use previously constructed instruments and others develop their own. All, however, should be careful to examine the selected questionnaires for relationships between items and programs goals, making sure that all the appropriate questions are asked.

In addition to surveys and questionnaires, program evaluators often use information from classroom observations to help determine effectiveness of the program and achievement of goals. Since most educators agree that gifted students can engage in activities requiring more application, analysis, synthesis, and evaluation earlier and to a greater degree than other students, the classroom interaction should reflect activity involving these processes. Several observation instruments have been developed to help delineate the kind and amount of interaction and activity that occur within the classroom. Evaluators, however, should select these observation instruments on the basis of the goals of the specific program being evaluated; otherwise the results will not help describe the relationship between goals and implementation, which is, after all, a major purpose of program evaluation. Also, the rating on observation instruments should be consistent from one rating session to another. If raters interpret the items differently, the evaluator will be unable to assess the classroom behavior accurately. Finally, the observations of the classroom should be conducted in situations that reflect typical teacher and student behavior and that allow for adequate observation time. If the situations are atypical or the time too short, the results of the observation may provide erroneous information that could lead to inaccurate conclusions. Consequently, when selecting an observation instrument, evaluators should be concerned with applicability of the instrument to measure stated goals, consistency of observations among different raters, and representativeness of the situations in which the observations occur.

SPECIAL PROBLEMS WITH STANDARDIZED TESTS

Often educators use standardized tests, especially achievement tests, as part of the evaluation procedure. Such use of these instruments, however, may create a distorted view of the program: first, because of the tests themselves, and second, because of statistical analysis of these tests. Standardized tests are usually designed for the general population and consequently are inappropriate for extreme groups, such as gifted students. The differences between the general population and the gifted are reflected in the number of questions designed for each group. While the tests contain many questions that distinguish among most students, they contain few that distinguish among gifted students. This, in turn, makes it difficult for an evaluator to compare results from one gifted group with those from another gifted group or, perhaps more importantly, to compare results from a pre- with those from a post-test situation for the same gifted group. Consequently, growth of students in a program for gifted and talented is difficult to determine using these tests.

In addition to the relatively low number of questions for this group, there is also relatively little room for improvement for gifted learners. For example, students who enter the program at the 98th or 99th percentile cannot improve very much. Furthermore, many questions on standardized tests are actually in conflict with some of the characteristics of the gifted. One common characteristic, for example, is the ability to see relationships among diverse ideas. While the test presumes one correct answer for a question, these students can often envision situations in which several of the "wrong" answers could be correct. This problem is discussed in greater length in *Characteristics and Identification of Gifted and Talented Students.*

Statistically, standardized tests also present difficulties. A phenomenon called "regression effect" makes it unlikely that individuals who score extremely high on a standardized test will show gains on the test. The regression effect, in brief, means that there is a statistical tendency for extremes to move toward the middle range on repeated measures. Individuals who score very high on a standardized test, for example, will tend to score closer to the mean when taking the test a second or third time. This phenomenon, of course, further complicates evaluation of improvement or gain using standardized tests as the major source of information about the program.

SUMMARY

When evaluating programs for the gifted and talented, evaluators should take into account several factors.

1. The evaluation should focus directly on the major goals of the specific program even though measurement of these goals may be more difficult and complex than that of specific objectives.
2. Since in most programs for the gifted the learning revolves around classroom activity and interaction, the evaluation procedure should include an observation and description of teacher and student behavior and the relationship between this behavior and the stated goals. This observation should focus directly on the goals and objectives of the specific program.
3. Evaluators should be cautious about relying too heavily on standardized tests because these tests are usually designed for

a different population. Although an increasing number of tests are being developed for gifted and talented, evaluators should examine them critically to determine the relationships among program goals, student characteristics, and test items as well as between the program and the norming populations. With these considerations, it is suggested that evaluators employ several procedures to give a clear picture of the program.

4. The evaluation should serve two functions:
   a. To continually modify the program to accomplish the goals more effectively
   b. To assess the overall relationship among program goals, student characteristics, identification procedures, and curriculum, ultimately evaluating the success of the program in attaining its goals.

Example

The program described in the following example is one designed for intellectually and academically gifted and talented fourth and fifth grade students. While the students are homogeneously grouped for their academic studies in self-contained classes, they are heterogeneously grouped for all other areas, such as homeroom and special subjects. The identification procedure involved used information from several sources, including teacher recommendations based on behavioral checklists, IQ and achievement tests, and peer and self-nomination. The general curriculum followed Tuttle's adaption of Renzulli's *Enrichment Triad Model* (see Chapter 3).

The program evaluator became involved with the program after the selection of students. In general, the purpose of the evaluation was to provide formative information during the year to modify strategies and curriculum when appropriate as well as to conduct a summative evaluation at the end of the academic year. Often, data gathered for the formative evaluation also helped draw conclusions for the summative report.

Early in the year the program evaluator and the curriculum coordinator explored a variety of questions that could be considered in the evaluation. After discussion with others, these questions were condensed as follows:

79

Attitudes

- Do parents of students in the program have a favorable attitude toward the program?
- Do teachers in general have a favorable attitude toward the program?
- Do students in and outside the program have a favorable attitude toward the program?

Curriculum

- Do the products of the students show superior abilities?
- Did the students acquire the basic skills and concepts taught in the regular program?
- Did the classroom activities reflect the program goals?
- Did the students in the program improve in ability to perform at the application and synthesis levels of Bloom's Taxonomy?
- In what ways was this program different from the regular program?

Consistency

- Were the various components of the program (goals, student characteristics, selection procedure, curriculum, and evaluation) consistent with each other?

To answer these questions the evaluator used several sources, including questionnaires, interviews, student products, classroom observations, and pre-post tests. In addition, he also analyzed the components of the program to determine consistency. As part of the formative evaluation, the teachers met periodically with the administrative staff and evaluator to discuss curriculum and student activities. To use the evaluation process as a learning experience for students, the evaluator had student committees develop questionnaires for parents, teachers, and other students. The summative evaluation included data from the pre-post tests, classroom observations, questionnaires, and interviews. In addition, the evaluator compared pre-post efforts between gifted and regular groups and between gifted in this program and gifted in other programs. The evaluator's final report to the school included an overview

Evaluation Procedure

	Attitudes Toward Program	Curriculum	Consistency of Components
Instruments	Questionnaires: • Parents of students in program • Parents of students not in program • Teachers in program • Teachers not in program • Students in program • Students not in program Interviews: • Students in program • Teachers in program	• Ross Test of Higher Cognitive Processes • Composition Test • Student Products • Checklist of basic skills and concepts • Florida Taxonomy of Cognitive Behavior (classroom observation) • Martinson-Weiner Rating Scale of Significant Behaviors in Teaching the Gifted (classroom observation)	• Chart of goals, characteristics, selection procedure, curriculum, and evaluation
Procedure	• Evaluation Committees (students) construct questionnaires • Evaluator interviews teachers and students • Evaluator analyzes responses in questionnaires (see previous discussion) and statements in interviews	• Pre-post administration of Ross and Composition Tests • Evaluator analysis of student products • Outside observation of classes • Comparison of gain scores on Ross and composition tests between control and program groups	• Evaluator analyzes chart for consistency

of goals and curricular approach, description of evaluation procedure, results by category and question, conclusions and recommendations, and samples of the instruments used. This report was written for school administrators and therefore included information of particular interest to them (4).

Evaluation of an Identification Procedure

For the past few years several program directors have requested that we assess the effectiveness of their identification procedures. To accomplish this we focused on the relationship between the procedure and performance in the specific program, examining each instrument and each item thereon in relation to individual performance within the program. The result in each case was a revised identification procedure composed of instruments and items designed for the particular program and intended population. While certainly more productive for the program itself, this procedure is limited in that it does not identify other areas of giftedness not recognized within the particular program. To do this, other programs and procedures would have to be designed.

References

1. Bloom, Benjamin S.; Hastings, J. Thomas; and Madaus, George F. *Handbook on Formative and Summative Evaluation of Student Learning.* New York: McGraw-Hill Book Co., 1971.
2. Renzulli, Joseph. *A Guidebook for Evaluating Programs for the Gifted and Talented.* Ventura, Calif.: Office of the Ventura County Superintendent of Schools, 1975.
3. Reynolds, M. C. "A Crisis in Evaluation." *Exceptional Children* 32 (May 1966): 585–92.
4. Tuttle, Frederick B., Jr. "Evaluation of Delphi Program." Greece Central School District. Greece, N.Y., 1979.
5. Williams, Maida B. "Evaluations of the A.L.A.P Identification Procedure." Warwick Public Schools (RI), 1983.
6. Williams, Maida B.; Tuttle, Frederick B., Jr., and Gallerani, David. "Evaluation of the Achievement of Individual Potential Identification Process." District III, Boston Public Schools, 1982.

Chapter 6
SUMMARY: QUESTIONS AND STEPS IN INITIATING A PROGRAM

QUESTIONS IN INITIATING A PROGRAM

When program developers begin to initiate a new program, they should be prepared to address several questions and issues. In the discussion of some of the more critical questions that follows, sample responses are provided where appropriate. Each situation is unique, however, and program developers should form their own responses to the questions to fit their particular grades, community, and school system. Some of the issues embedded in these questions have been discussed earlier; they are highlighted again because of their importance.

General Questions

The following are general questions that may be raised by parents, other members of the community, teachers, or administrators about the overall reason for a special program and its effect on the community, school, and students.

1. *Why is a special program for gifted and talented necessary?*

Many students in our country are not receiving instruction commensurate with their abilities, interests, and characteristics. While some attention has been focused on handicapped and learning-disabled individuals and much has been done for the average learner through teacher training and textbook publishing, the gifted and talented students have received very little program recognition and support. Usually these students spend most of their time in school in frustration—receiving information, instruction, and materials far below their potential and inappropriate for their characteristics. In most classroom situations they are presented with concepts and skills they have already mastered; consequently, much of their academic experience is repetitious, unnecessary, and unsatisfying. They need special attention and provision just as any other learners whose characteristics and abilities differ from those for whom most instruction is designed.

2. *Won't these students become an elitist group if they are singled out?*

This is a complex question that raises the issues of elitism, emotional problems, and social implications discussed previously. However, it is one that is usually asked in one form or another in every program for gifted and talented. The direct answer is, "In general, no, they won't." Research has been conducted in this area and the findings indicate that in most situations gifted and talented individuals in special programs do not consider themselves an elite group, nor do they have severe emotional problems. Gifted individuals in special programs realize they have exceptional abilities but are usually able to put them into realistic perspective.

Special programs for gifted and talented do not create emotional problems. Indeed, these problems may be avoided or alleviated by instituting a special program for the gifted since more emotional difficulties tend to arise from frustrating situations. Ruth Martinson reports research indicating that gifted and talented in special programs relate better to other individuals than gifted and talented not in these situations (1).

3. *How does the establishment of a program for gifted and talented relate to the school's philosophy?*

Most school systems have the ultimate goal of educating each student to fulfill the individual's potential. In addition, many also believe that instruction should be based as much on an individual's own needs and abilities as on the course content. The establishment of a program for the gifted and talented helps fulfill this obligation because it provides a specific group of learners who have special characteristics, needs, and abilities with the opportunity to fulfill their potential in a learning situation designed to meet their needs.

4. *What are the goals of the program for gifted and talented?*

The answer to this question will vary with each situation, depending on area of giftedness, curriculum, community, and philosophy. In general, most programs for gifted and talented have cited as goals the development of some of the following abilities:

- Leadership qualities such as self-awareness, social awareness, responsibility, and independence
- Advanced communication skills in a variety of areas
- Higher-level thinking skills (e.g., analysis, synthesis, and evaluation)
- Creative and productive thinking skills
- Problem-finding and problem-solving skills
- Independent research skills.

Although most of these goals also apply to other programs, they are often primary with the gifted and talented, while acquisition of skills and content usually takes precedence in regular classes (See question 12.)

5. *What is the school doing now to provide for the gifted?*

This question also has several issues embedded in it, such as current program and individualizing instruction within the classroom. At the middle and high school levels some schools have instituted honors and advanced placement programs. Many consider these classes as programs for the gifted and talented. In most situations, however, such classes do not provide for gifted individuals because they are not often based on their characteristics, needs, and abilities. Rather, they may have the students work in the same manner as in other classes, stressing knowledge and recall of information, albeit with more advanced materials at a faster rate. Although they are good programs for the bright student, they are usually inappropriate for the gifted and talented individual. In any case, the program developer should be aware of these classes, the materials used, and the type of instruction before claiming the need to establish a new program.

At the elementary school level, many view "individual instruction" as the way in which the needs of the gifted and talented have been met in the school. Ideally this technique should provide the appropriate instruction for all students, including the gifted. However, it seldom does. As Ruth Martinson observes:

> Even though individualized instruction accommodates the gifted and talented to a greater degree than the traditional classroom operation, it cannot replace separate programs which expose the students to learnings that exist beyond the confines of even the best individually instructed classroom. (1)

Furthermore, few classroom teachers have been trained to identify and work with the gifted. Often they provide for these students by allowing them to do more of the same or by having them work with less able classmates. While the latter method may facilitate some of the individualization within the classroom, it does not help the gifted and talented individuals work to their abilities and develop their skills.

Finally, many school administrators state they do not have programs for the gifted and talented. They frequently overlook varsity sports, however. These sports programs fulfill many of the criteria for gifted programs, having established a careful screening procedure, a special, high-level curriculum, and high expectations of the entrants. Some developers have used the example of varsity sports to illustrate the existence of special programs for gifted and talented in school systems in which administrators stated they were philosophically opposed to programs for the gifted.

6. *How will the program affect the rest of the school?*

All administrators and teachers raise this question either publicly or privately. In general, a program for gifted and talented has a positive effect on the total school system. By providing for these students, the school alleviates their frustration and discontent and, since these are often the real student leaders, creates a positive atmosphere throughout the student body. The curricular changes in classes for gifted and talented often affect the curriculum in other classes as new resources are brought into the school, products and projects are shared, and different techniques are tried.

These benefits, however, will occur only if opportunities for interaction and involvement among faculty exist. Otherwise, there may be some resentment of the special program and a negative atmosphere may result. This interaction should be encouraged by early involvement and awareness of all teachers and staff and by continual sharing of ideas and resources throughout the school. The key is articulation among teachers and staff.

Other effects on the school will depend on the specific program design. If the design calls for a school within a school as in Brockton, Massachusetts, the overall organization of that school will be affected. On the other hand, a mentor program conducted outside the school may have little effect on other classes. If students are removed from classes on a permanent basis, the daily classroom routine will not be altered so much as it would be in a program where students are removed from some classes for part of the time. These effects have to be considered because ultimately the attitudes of individual teachers who may have to cope with them will greatly influence the overall program success.

7. *How are some other school systems providing for their gifted and talented students?*

This may be one of the most important questions since ultimately the school system is responsible to the community it serves and must respond to its reactions. Therefore, it is vital for program developers to consider the community and the means to ensure a generally positive reaction to the program. One way to help this effort is to involve members of the community throughout the process. Members may represent parent groups as well as local organizations that might become involved later in the program (e.g., community theater, local business). Teachers in the program should be encouraged to continue this involvement and community awareness after the program has been established.

Another group of parents is equally vital to the establishment and success of the program: those whose children are not involved in the program for the gifted and talented. Members of this group can become very vocal in their opposition to the program if they believe it is affecting their children adversely. Since they, by definition, constitute the majority, their concern must be addressed before the opposition becomes too strong. Several of their potential concerns have been considered previously, but one major question remains: How does the school cope with parents who feel their children should be in the program but are not? *First,* the criteria for selection must be carefully defined. This does not mean

87

only tests should be used, but rather that program developers should know the relationship between the criteria, the characteristics, and the curriculum. As Ruth Martinson observes:

> A program tailored to the gifted and talented but applied to the average causes frustration and failure for the average; conversely, a program designed for the average and made available for the gifted and talented restricts self-fulfillment for the gifted and talented and can also cause frustration and failure for the gifted. (1)

Second, the school must decide how pressure for admission will be handled. Will some students who have influential parents be admitted while others are kept out? Or will any children be allowed into the program on a trial basis? If the latter, the criteria for continuing in or dropping out of the program should be made clear. These factors do not have to be clarified immediately, but they should be addressed for later development.

8. How do others feel about establishing a program for the gifted and talented in their school system?

Before making a proposal for the development of a program for gifted and talented, various attitudes toward such a program on an informal basis should be explored. By discussing the need for the program on an informal basis with individuals from groups such as the school board, teachers' association, parents' organization, student government, and influential administrators, program developers can often foresee potential conflicts and enlist valuable support. This information helps the administration decide whether or not to begin work on developing the program.

Implementation

The following questions address specific aspects of implementing the program in the school; they often arise during an initial discussion with a chief administrator or a school board.

9. How many students will be involved?

The response to this question, of course, depends on several factors, such as type of program, characteristics of population within the community, size of student body, and number of grade levels involved. The most legitimate approach would be to work from the criteria for selection within a specific area and accept all students who meet these criteria. Then, the program would have to be developed around that number. If it is to be at a single grade level for a full-time teacher, the program might involve combining grade levels or hiring a part-time teacher.

The foregoing approach is the most valid way of determining numbers, but many times people want an estimate of potential figures before the criteria have been established. Depending on the type of program and the characteristics of the community, a gifted and talented program may involve up to 10 percent of the potential population. For example, if a school plans to institute a program encompassing grades three and four in a nongraded situation and has 150 students at each grade for a total of 300 potential candidates, approximately 15 students will be involved if they assume 5 percent of this population is gifted and talented.

Some schools work from the other direction. They assume a program needs a minimal number of students for implementation and then base final numbers on that figure. For example, if the program involves a full-time teacher and the system needs 20 students to warrant the teacher, then at least 20 gifted students will have to be identified. While this method may be practical logistically, it may be unrealistic in terms of the individuals who actually meet the criteria for the program.

10. *How will the program be staffed?*

Again, the response to this question depends on the type of program envisioned. Program developers should, however, be aware of some of the staffing options that will help meet the goals of the program. These may range from full-time faculty in a separate school to resource people from the community in a mentor program. In each case selection and training should be considered. The selection should be in accordance with local teacher association and administrative policy; it should, in addition, focus on interest in working with gifted and talented, expertise in the field, training in education of the gifted and talented, as well as other teacher characteristics mentioned in Chapter 4.

In-service training is also a necessary component. Consequently, program developers should be aware of the areas of training needed and the means of accomplishing it. Some training may be conducted in general through a local college or university that offers courses in educating the gifted and talented or through leadership workshops conducted by various organizations. Sometimes specific training is provided by a consultant in gifted and talented who will gear the training to a specific program and may, on a long-term arrangement, work with teachers in their classes as well as with administrative designs, curriculum, and evaluation. Where neither courses nor consultation is available, self-help tests might provide some basic training for teachers. (See Selected References—*Star Power*, and Treffinger and Curl.) In-service work might well encompass the entire faculty since an effective program will require cooperation and support throughout the school.

11. *How will students be selected for the program?*

Although some educators have designed general identification procedures for gifted and talented, each program should have an identification procedure that reflects the characteristics of the potential population, the goals of the program, and the curriculum within that program. After these elements are considered, the program developers may find other identification procedures to be appropriate, but they should not be adopted unless they fit the particular situation.

With that caution, program developers can respond to this question once the general type of program has been determined. *Characteristics and Identification of Gifted and Talented Students* lists general approaches for selecting students for programs within each of these categories: intellectual, academic, visual and performing arts, creative and productive thinking. Program developers should know the kinds of instruments and procedures they plan to use because these factors will affect the cost and the amount of staff involvement, as well as the time for the selection process.

12. *What should be taught?*

Ultimately someone must ask about the content of a special program for gifted and talented and how it will differ from other classes. Many educators suggest that any program for the gifted must be qualitatively different from the regular program in the school. Although there are several different definitions of "qualitative difference," in general this difference will be reflected in content, instruction, and student product. The difference in most situations is one of level and quality rather than quantity. Instead of having students in the program do more with the same materials, these students should be using materials and methods that are appropriate to their level. Instruction in academic programs, for example, should stress higher levels of cognition (see Chapter 3), such as analysis and synthesis, more than lower levels, such as recall of information.

The difference is not that the pupils in the special program work at higher levels only and those in regular classes are confined to work at lower levels. All students should receive instruction at all levels, but in programs for the gifted a greater percentage of instruction should be at higher levels.

Finally, the difference between programs should be reflected in the quality of work the learners produce. While students in programs for gifted and talented should receive instruction in and have experiences with a wide variety of appropriate skills, such as problem finding and problem solving, ultimately they should produce works that reflect their superior abilities in a particular area.

In addition to qualitative difference between programs, parents, teachers, and administrators are also concerned with the acquisition of "basic" skills in these special programs. Developers should ensure that students will possess all the skills basic to the various curriculum areas as they proceed through the program.

One individual responded to this question in the following manner: In the special classes for the gifted and talented our program will have a high percentage of instruction at higher levels of cognition, emphasis on creative and productive thinking skills, and work with problem-solving and problem-finding skills. Although these areas are often stressed in regular classes, in the special classes teachers will spend a greater amount of time and effort on them. In addition, the acquisition of "basic" skills will be ensured but not stressed so heavily as in other classes. Finally, a great deal of emphasis will be placed on high quality of student product and depth of research involved in the production. We would not hold these expectations of students in the regular curriculum.

---

13. *What support services will be needed to implement the program?*

Most programs will require periodic input from a variety of services throughout the school system. When a program is under consideration, these services have to be taken into account as they will affect other areas such as cost, other programs, and community. In programs for the gifted and talented, for example, school psychologists might help with the identification and counseling, bus drivers might be needed for additional transportation, or parents might be asked to serve as mentors.

In addition to these areas that are usually viewed as support services, program developers should also examine the need for input from teachers outside the special program. Some of these might be content area teachers who serve as mentors or who help identify students for the program. Others might involve art and music teachers in helping students with special projects. While this involvement may be extremely valuable, it should be foreseen early since it will require extra time and effort from these individuals.

14. *How much will the program cost?*

The answers to the previous questions will affect the cost of implementing the program, and ultimately the establishment of the program may depend on the estimated cost. If the program developers have an estimate of the cost or at least the variables that will have to be considered, realistic decisions can be made early to provide for the most productive work. In general, the following factors are often considered: teacher salary, transportation, in-service release time, consultation, identification materials, instructional materials, and room rental. Depending on the design, many of these expenses may be absorbed within the regular budget by reorganizing resources already in the system. For example, if the design is for a self-contained, homogeneous class of twenty-five students, the cost of the teacher would not be additional as the school would need a teacher for those students with or without the special program. If parent volunteers will provide transportation, this charge may be reduced. Cost should not be viewed unrealistically, however, because the saving of some money may jeopardize the effectiveness of the program. For example, some schools have attempted to save money by not providing in-service training and awareness for the faculty. While money was saved initially, the programs were endangered because of lack of awareness throughout the school system, with consequent arousal of suspicions.

15. What about continuity through the system?

Even though most new programs are initiated at a single grade level, program developers should also plan for future expansion. Programs for gifted and talented that are discontinuous, abandoning students before the end of their schooling, are incomplete. One student in a program that terminated at ninth grade commented, "Now I don't have to do much work until twelfth grade. I've already done what they do in tenth and eleventh grades." Establishing a program for the gifted should indicate the recognition of the need to provide special experiences for these students at all grade levels, developing their skills and abilities in a coordinated, sequential manner.

A parent at a parent-support group meeting was concerned with future development. His oldest child is eight and in third grade. He suggested that rather than having third graders' parents working for programs to be initiated a year too late, perhaps they should be looking at high school programs to pave the way for the future.

---

16. How will the effectiveness of the program be evaluated?

Responding initially to the method of evaluation, program developers might explain when the evaluation could take place, which elements would be considered, and who should conduct the evaluation. As indicated in Chapter 5, program evaluation should be an ongoing process as well as a final assessment. This continuing aspect should be initiated early in order that the entire program development may be examined. When designing a method to evaluate a program, all components, including goals, selection process, curriculum, and evaluation, should be taken into account. Finally, the evaluator, whether a consultant or a committee, should be designated early to provide for total involvement in the program development process from the beginning.

17. *Who will have responsibility for the program?*

The question of responsibility is sometimes unresolved until it is assumed by neglect. No one else takes it; consequently, the teacher is left with the total responsibility for the program. This places the teacher in the awkward position of implementer, evaluator, and public relations representative. Without a formal assignment of responsibility for various functions, misinformation may be conveyed and a frustrating situation may arise. Often the duties are divided among various individuals, with the teacher responsible for classroom activities and student evaluation, the building principal taking care of public relations, the curriculum coordinator in charge of general curriculum development and continuity, and an outside consultant assuming the responsibility for in-service training and program evaluation.

STEPS IN INITIATING A PROGRAM

The following fifteen steps for developing a program for the gifted parallel the preceding questions. Both encompass suggestions by several educators in this field, especially William Vassar, Consultant for Gifted and Talented in Connecticut. Although the word "steps" implies a sequential progression, developers should not proceed in a linear fashion. Rather, they should consider several "steps" simultaneously, moving back and forth among them as ideas are clarified, and often jumping ahead to gain insights necessary for "earlier" steps.

1. *Establishing the need.* Why does this particular school or community need a special program for gifted and talented? Can't these students do well enough on their own? Hasn't the school already provided them with honors and advanced placement programs?

2. *Stating goals and objectives.* What do we hope the students will gain from participating in this program? How will they demonstrate their growth?

3. *Delineating the population.* What area(s) of gifted and talented will be considered for the program? What are the characteristics of individuals to be included? How many students and what grade levels might the program involve?

94

4. *Establishing selective criteria.* What instruments and procedures are available to help locate individuals with these special characteristics? What will be the criteria for admission? Will the approach be inclusive or exclusive? How much will the selection procedure cost? How long will it take? What staff will be involved? Will staff require in-service training?

5. *Describing staffing needs.* How many teachers will be needed for instruction? What qualifications will be required? Will teachers need auxiliary support from aides, counselors, and/or parents?

6. *Describing physical facilities.* How many rooms will be involved? When will these rooms be used? Does the program call for special instructional or laboratory materials? Will extra transportation be required?

7. *Describing in-service training.* What special training should be received by staff directly involved in the program? Will in-service workshops be necessary for teachers and administrators outside the program? Who should provide this training? Will there be programs for parents and community? When should in-service training sessions occur?

8. *Detailing administrative design.* What will the overall structure of the program involve? How does this design facilitate the achievement of the goals? How much will it cost beyond the regular program?

9. *Developing curriculum.* What are the specific objectives of instruction? What model(s) will provide a theoretical basis for instruction? How will the curriculum for the gifted and talented differ from that in the regular program? How will the "basic curriculum" be acquired by students in the special program? Who will develop the curriculum? Will they need extra help?

10. *Listing community resources.* How does the program involve the community? What resources, including people, places, and activities, are available to benefit the program? What resources are available inside the school, including staff, places, and extracurricular activities?

11. *Exploring sources of funding.* What financial support is available within the established budget? Can some money be saved by

reallocating resources? What external financial or resource support is available, including grants and donations of material and/or space? Can the students raise money for special projects?

12. *Describing the program evaluation procedure.* How will evaluation be conducted? Will it be both formative and summative? What kind of information will be of interest to whom? Who will receive the evaluation? Who will conduct the evaluation? When will the program evaluator become involved in the program?

13. *Delineating roles.* Who will be responsible for various aspects of the program? Who will have overall control and responsibility?

14. *Describing necessary consultation.* What outside expertise will be helpful? Who will need this help? When should it be made available? How much will it cost?

15. *Delineating the articulation procedure.* How and when will information about the program be shared among the teachers? How much opportunity will teachers in the program have to interact with teachers outside the program? How and when will administrators share information and ideas about the program with faculty? How and when will the school share information about the program with the community? Who will assume responsibility to ensure articulation?

Recommended Phases of Program Development

Perrone, Morris-Jones, and Post of the University of Wisconsin at Madison have listed tasks that should occur within a given time line to institute a program for gifted and talented.

Phase I

- Identify a coordinator.
- Appoint a Parent Advisory Committee and a Professional Steering Committee
- Develop philosophy, goals, and objectives.
- Design program with differentiated content, techniques, materials, and learning environments consistent with philosophy, goals, and objectives.
- Begin workshops and in-service meetings with administrators, teachers, and other school personnel.

- Identify teachers of gifted and talented.
- Design assessment schedule and identify procedures to be used.
- Begin regular staff meetings.
- Orient parents and students to program goals and student needs.
- Collect and develop relevant curriculum materials.
- Plan pre- and post-evaluative materials for program.

Phase II

- Organize Community Resource Catalogue (persons, organizations, places, and experiences).
- Designate resource centers and a resource person at each school.
- Develop case conference materials and procedures so students can: (1) be identified and (2) be programmed according to their educational needs.
- Continue regular public dissemination of information.
- Meet with teachers at each school to discuss who and why identification of each child.
- Meet regularly with parents of the gifted and talented students.
- Continue screening new arrivals in the district.
- Curriculum personnel and teachers of gifted and talented classes prepare a written curriculum. (2)

References

1. Martinson, Ruth A. "Research on the Gifted and Talented: Its Implications for Education." In *Education of the Gifted and Talented: Report to the Congress of the United States by the U.S. Commissioner of Education.* Washington, D.C.: Government Printing Office, 1972.
2. Perrone, Philip A.; Morris-Jones, Dana; and Post, Phyllis. "Procedures in Programming for Talented Students." Madison: Guidance Institute for Talented Students, University of Wisconsin-Madison, n.d.

SUPPLEMENTARY MATERIALS

GLOSSARY OF ADMINISTRATIVE DESIGNS

ACCELERATION. Selected students are allowed to advance more quickly than chronological peers. This may be accomplished in several ways: early admission, grade skipping, compressing curricula. This approach has been especially successful in areas such as mathematics where the learning is sequential and hierarchical in nature.

ADVANCED PLACEMENT. Students in high school take courses that allow them to bypass some courses in college. In some situations students may take college courses in high school and receive college credit for them.

CLUSTER GROUPING. Teachers from different disciplines have classes with the same groups of selected students. Often they have responsibility for designing schedules as well as curriculum. This design is usually found at the middle or junior high school level.

DIFFERENTIATED CURRICULUM. Groups of students have unique learning characteristics in degree if not in kind and, consequently, require instructional programs different from those offered in regular programs. The differentiated curriculum is based on the singular needs and characteristics of the particular group and should be of primary concern when developing any educational program for a specific group of students.

ENRICHMENT. Students are often given opportunities to participate in activities beyond the basic curriculum. This enriched curriculum either supplements regular work or allows students to extend their skills and learnings in new directions. Enrichment often involves special projects or individual or small group learning activities.

EXTRACURRICULAR CLUBS. Students with particular interests form a club with a faculty sponsor and explore areas within that field after school.

INDEPENDENT STUDY. Selected students are allowed to pursue an area of interest apart from the rest of their class. Often this results in an extensive project based on a contractual agreement between teacher and student.

INDIVIDUALIZED INSTRUCTION. Each student has an individually designed course of study to meet particular needs, abilities, and characteristics. Special materials such as kits and self-correcting programs are often used to facilitate the instruction.

IQ. While often confused with actual intelligence, an individual's IQ, or intelligence quotient, is a score reflecting the comparison of one's chronological age and one's score on a special test. Many areas of intelligence (e.g., creativity) are not recognized by an IQ score.

ITINERANT TEACHER. A trained teacher conducts classes for gifted and talented students at different schools. Usually there are pullout, supplemental classes in which the students are periodically excused from regular classes to work with this teacher.

MAGNET SCHOOLS. Some larger systems have provided for gifted and talented by transporting them to a separate school where the entire curriculum is designed for their characteristics and areas of superior ability.

MENTORS. Students are paired with members of the community who have expertise in the area of interest of the selected students. Usually they meet with each other after school or on weekends, with the work being supplementary to the regular curriculum.

RESOURCE CENTER. An area is set aside with a teacher trained to work with gifted and talented students. The students may meet with the teacher informally during the day or at specific times during the week to supplement their other classes. Sometimes selected students from other schools in the district are transported to this center for special, supplemental classes.

SATURDAY AND SUMMER EXPERIENCES. Some gifted and talented students expand their abilities by enrolling in special summer or Saturday programs. These may be run by the school system, by an outside organization, such as a college, an individual or a private concern, or by a nonprofit organization.

SCHOOLS WITHIN SCHOOLS. When the population does not warrant an entire building and faculty to accommodate the gifted and talented, school systems sometimes set aside part of a school for these students. Although the gifted may have their academic experience as a homogeneous group, they may have other classes with the rest of the school.

SELF-CONTAINED, HOMOGENEOUS CLASS. Students are placed with other students showing similar characteristics for their academic experiences. The class may be at one grade level or may combine grades. One teacher is responsible for the class. This arrangement works especially well at the elementary level.

TEAM TEACHING. An adaptation of cluster grouping, this design enables two teachers to cooperate in scheduling and planning by giving them the same selected students for part of the day. They often try to integrate their subjects into an interdisciplinary program.

ROLES OF INVOLVED PERSONNEL*

Coordinator	Teacher	Student	Principal	Parent
• Design, develop, coordinate, & evaluate the program.	• Provide an enriched individualized program for the gifted.	• Attend regular or specially scheduled programs or events.	• Become knowledgeable about the unique needs of the gifted.	• Provide support & stimulation at home.
• Develop & implement curriculum (techniques, materials) related to enriching the total program.	• Assist students in planning, organizing, & evaluating tasks.	• Complete selected tasks.	• Become acquainted with gifted students in the school.	• Become mentor for gifted children.
• Prepare financial, statistical, & descriptive reports as needed to develop, maintain, & account for the program.	• Screen, develop, & provide appropriate materials for the gifted.	• Communicate & share learning experiences with peers, teachers, & parents.	• Stimulate interest in & concern for the gifted.	• Enlist the support of community members who can serve as resource persons for the gifted, & provide unique learning experiences for gifted pupils.
• Coordinate identification & certification procedures.	• Evaluate pupil progress.	• Practice decision-making skills.	• Urge teachers to provide qualitatively-differentiated programs for the gifted in their classrooms.	• Become member of a Parent Advisory Council or other decision-making group.
• Serve as consultant & resource to the staff, students, & parents involved with the program.	• Interpret the program to parents.	• Develop self-awareness & understanding.	• Encourage & assist teachers in securing appropriate instructional materials for the gifted.	
• Participate as part of the Educational Services staff.	• Provide an enriched extension of the regular curriculum for gifted students in intra- or extra-classroom settings.	• Participate in planning & evaluating learning experiences within the program.	• Work cooperatively with other personnel in objectively evaluating the program.	
• Promote public relations activities at the local, county, & state levels.	• Demonstrate diverse methods of instruction appropriate for the gifted, such as problem solving, independent study, etc.			

* From "Identification of Talented Students" by Philip A. Perrone et al., Guidance Institute for Talented Students, University of Wisconsin-Madison, n.d.

DIFFERENTIATING CURRICULUM
FOR THE GIFTED AND TALENTED*

Curriculum for the gifted and talented can only be marked as such if it encompasses elements which distinguish it from being suitable for the education of *all* children. Curriculum for gifted students must be congruent with the characteristics that identify them as a distinct population. The answer to the question of why a student is gifted or talented is also the answer to the question of what type of curricular provisions should be developed for this child.

Differentiation of curricular activities for the gifted and talented relies on the elaboration of certain variables: procedures for presenting learning opportunities, nature of the input, and expectancies for learning outcomes.

DIFFERENTIATING LEARNING WITHIN THE REGULAR CURRICULUM

Procedures for Presenting Learning Opportunities		
	Exposure	—Students are exposed to experiences, materials, and information which are outside the bounds of the regular curriculum, do not match age/grade expectancies, and introduce something new or unusual.
	Extension	—Students are afforded opportunities to elaborate on the regular curriculum through additional allocation of working time, materials, and experiences, and/or further self-initiated or related study.
	Development	—Students are provided with instruction which focuses on thorough or new explanation of a concept or a skill which is part of a general learning activity within the regular curriculum.

DIFFERENTIATING LEARNING AS A SEPARATE CURRICULUM

Type of Input	
	Accelerated or advanced content
	Higher degree of complexity of content
	Introduction of content beyond the prescribed curriculum
	Student-selected content according to interest
	Working with the abstract concepts in a content area
	Level of resources used
	Type of resources available

Expectancies for Learning	
	Appropriating a longer time for learning
	Creating or generating something new (information, ideas, product)
	Depth of learning
	Transfer and application of learning to other and/or new areas of greater challenge
	Evidence of personal growth or sophistication in attitudes, appreciations, feelings
	Formulating new generalizations
	Development of higher level cognitive processes
	Stylizing and implementing own study design

---

*SOURCE: *Providing Programs for the Gifted and Talented: A Handbook* by Sandra N. Kaplan, pp. 123-26 (Ventura, Calif.: N/S-LTI-G/T, 1974).

Differentiating Curricular Activities
for the Gifted and Talented

Means of Differentiating	Explanation	Illustration
1. Accelerated or advanced content	Working with knowledge and skills which correlate with the student's mental rather than chronological age, parallel his interests, and satisfy his need and quest for substantive information	Student ready for algebra at nine-year-old level is given a tutor.
2. Higher degree of complexity of content	Allowing student performance to dictate speed/direction of learning Learning experiences which require higher order thinking processes, such as analyzing, creating, and evaluating Learning experiences that require assimilation of principles, theories, and concepts associated with knowledge held by "the professional or expert"	The gifted student is pursuing the topic of Occults as an outgrowth of learning the expected topic of Mythology.
3. Introduction of content beyond the prescribed curriculum	Learning what is traditionally reserved for another grade or age level Learning what is related to other areas or crosses the boundaries of the disciplines	Gifted student is studying the cause-and-effect relationships of various forms of paternalism in people's voting pattern in different countries as an independent study within a United States history class.
4. Student-selected content according to interest	Allowing student need and interest to govern what is to be learned and/or to dictate what areas within a body of knowledge that will be studied	The gifted student interested in violin is independently pursuing the topic in a general music class by leaving his regular class in the elementary school to attend class at the high school.
5. Working with the abstract concepts in a content area	Dealing with those ideas, theories, and concepts which are inferred or discrete and which require reflective, critical, and creative thinking in order to make them concrete or give them meaning	The gifted student illustrates the ways a proverb is "lived" by a literary character.

Differentiating Curricular Activities
for the Gifted and Talented (Continued)

Means of Differentiating	Explanation	Illustration
6. Level of resources	Allowing students to use resources beyond those reserved or designated for regular curriculum input	Gifted elementary student calls a college professor to obtain information regarding his questions in a particular subject.
7. Type of resources available	Insisting on acquiring information from multiple and varied resources which includes other informational sources besides books	The gifted student was given the yellow page telephone directory to find out who could be contacted to assist him in obtaining information regarding his study.
8. Appropriating a longer time for learning	Acknowledging that the student with multi-interests and abilities needs appropriate time to learn by defining his work schedule; recognizing that the student sometimes needs to pursue a topic or skill more extensively or to a greater degree of proficiency	The gifted student contracts with the teacher as a means of setting time limits on studying a topic. The gifted student is given additional time to experiment with properties in chemistry in order to discover or prove something in which he is interested in a more complex manner than is assigned to the other students in the class.
9. Creating or generating something new	Expressing additional examples, new and original alternatives and relationships, and possible solutions in either verbal or illustrative form to given issues, problems, and ideas	The gifted student, as a result of a study of current political issues, is developing a new method to raise campaign funds for political office which is to be submitted to a Congressman for reaction.
10. Depth of learning providing alternative and related experience with recognition that the student requires fewer stages and less time to learn a concept	Gathering information to a level of understanding which satisfies the attainment of a skill or idea, the quest for learning exhibited by the student and the objectives of the instructor	The gifted student is engaged in collecting and processing data which could clarify the meaning of loneliness as it applies to ethnic groups within American society.
11. Transfer and application of learning to other and/or new areas of greater challenge	Applying what is learned to substantiate, negate, extend, or verify learnings in another area of the curriculum or another body of knowledge	The gifted student in a math study is utilizing the process of multiplication to develop statistical predictions of how the country's food supply will accommodate the population explosion.

Differentiating Curricular Activities
for the Gifted and Talented (Continued)

Means of Differentiating	Explanation	Illustration
12. Evidence of personal growth or sophistication in attitude, appreciations, feelings	Cultivating and rewarding honest opinions and reactions, divergent responses, and questioning attitudes; incorporating learning about humaneness as a concomitant to learning a body of knowledge of a specific skill; learning how to assess and obtain feedback about "in" personal and academic endeavors	The gifted student is making a profile of famous men who were scholars in order to identify the traits he has in common with them.
13. Formulating new generalizations	Summarizing and developing new theories and ideas for what has been learned and which may be used at some other time.	The gifted student has summarized all the data relative to World War I and II to formulate a new theory about a society's need for dominance.
14. Development of higher-level cognitive processes	Learning and practicing the skills related to the processes of analyzing, synthesizing, and evaluating as both separate processes and as processes which are part of the strategies of problem solving, critical thinking, and creativity	The gifted student has evaluated the need for learning about geology and presented his argument to the Board of Education.
15. Stylizing and implementing a student study design	Recognizing and utilizing the skills of research and scientific exploration effectively in a given learning endeavor and finding out what style of learning is successful for the student	The gifted student has organized an outline for developing a position paper on some aspect of the use of atoms.

EVALUATING DIFFERENTIATED ACTIVITIES

Often, differentiation encompasses three areas: higher cognitive thinking skills, advanced general skills, and/or advanced content skills. To be sure, there are many other areas of differentiation, but these seem to be frequently cited and therefore usually in need of evaluation.

When examining higher cognitive skills, the program evaluator should attempt to determine how much class activity is devoted to work at the higher levels of analysis, synthesis, and evaluation. The assumption underlying programs with higher cognitive skills as a point of differentiation is that students will devote most of their class activity to these levels and accomplish work at the lower levels of knowledge and comprehension independently. The evaluation of this differentiation is based on the degree to which this assumption is met. It may be accomplished through observation using instruments such as the Florida Taxonomy of Educational Objectives, by student questionnaires, or by examination of teacher plans.

The second area of differentiation encompasses instruction in advanced general skills. These often include areas such as critical thinking, problem solving, and creative thinking. Programs that operate outside the general curriculum often stress instruction in advanced general skills as opposed to instruction in developmental skills that students receive in their general classes. To assess effectiveness of this differentiation, the evaluator first needs a clear picture of what these advanced skills are and how students are expected to demonstrate their acquisition. Then, the task is to judge whether or not students do indeed demonstrate acquisition of the designated advanced skills.

The third area of differentiation sometimes encompasses instruction in advanced content skills. This kind of differentiation is most prevalent in programs in which students have the "gifted" experience in a specific content area such as English, math, science, or social studies, in lieu of the general class. The advanced skills should be determined on the basis of the expectations within the general curriculum. For example, in English the major focus of the general curriculum might be on plot development and character. In the gifted program the advanced skills might include drawing relationships among methods of character delineation or between character development and theme. To assess the effectiveness of this differentiation, the evaluator needs to know the specific advanced content skills, the relationship between the advanced and the general skills, and how students are expected to demonstrate acquisition of the advanced skills in the specific content area.

106

SAMPLE PROGRAM GUIDELINES

The following program guidelines were developed for the Boston Public Schools to help teachers and developers design and implement gifted programs in Boston.* In District III, where they were initially used, the knowledge of the parameters within which we had to work was very beneficial. While these are not appropriate guidelines for all programs, some initial statement of parameters is helpful.

The following are components which should be included in the final description of a program for gifted and talented students in District III.

1. *Rationale:* The basic assumptions underlying the TAG program in District III are:

   1.1 Gifted and talented students should be able to engage in differentiated experiences based on their characteristics.

   1.2 All students, regardless of language, cultural, or economic background, should be considered for involvement in the TAG program to accommodate students from bilingual, multicultural, and varied socioeconomic communities.

   1.3 Acceptance in the TAG program should be based on behavioral characteristics of individuals within the framework of both program and cultural expectations.

2. *Goals and Objectives:* TAG programs in District III will specify objectives within the following goals:

   Students selected for the TAG program will:

   2.1 Produce quality products reflecting ability.

   2.2 Demonstrate abilities to synthesize information from a variety of sources and draw appropriate generalizations.

   2.3 Demonstrate acquisition of advanced skills in areas of research, creative and productive thinking, and various areas of communication.

   2.4 Work independently or in small groups in areas of personal concern.

   2.5 Demonstrate acquisition of essential skills as delineated by the District for specific grade levels and content areas.

---

*Adapted from "Guidelines for Program Design," by Frederick B. Tuttle, Jr. District III, Boston Public Schools, March 3, 1980.

3. *Administrative Design:* Administrative designs for individual schools may take any of several forms depending on teacher attitudes, school organization and resources, and student needs. The only designs which would be inappropriate would be those which require extensive grouping, prohibit participation in the program of some individuals (e.g., after school), or violate basic policies of the District.

4. *Characteristics of Target Population:* The specific characteristics of the population to be selected for participation in the District TAG programs will vary depending on the specific program designs and curricular models within the individual schools. In general, however, some of the following traits are characteristic of gifted and talented students to be considered for TAG programs in District III:

Curiosity
Ability to synthesize information from a variety of sources
Divergent thinking
Persistent in pursuit of interests
Ability to communicate ideas effectively
Critical of self and others
Perceptive

5. *Identification Procedure:* Although specific procedures will vary depending on components and needs at particular schools, each will work within the following parameters:

5.1 Identification will be based on behavioral characteristics reflective of cultural expectations and program and curricular requirements.

5.2 Test scores and academic achievement will compose only part of the identification procedure.

5.3 Identification instruments and criteria will be generally designed to include students who may be gifted within the framework of the program and curriculum rather than to exclude students who may not be gifted.

5.4 The identification procedure will reflect the total cultural make-up of the community, allowing each student an opportunity to be selected for the TAG program.

5.5 All parent inventories will be translated into the primary language of the students in the school.

6. *Curricular Approach:* While the specific curriculum will vary from one school to another, each TAG program should provide a curriculum which will:

6.1 Not penalize students who have been admitted to the program on the basis of potential but have not yet fulfilled that potential.

6.2 Be differentiated from the curriculum for other students.

6.3 Help identified students develop specific advanced skills and concepts.

6.4 Provide opportunities for intensive investigation of personal interests.

6.5 Encourage students to synthesize information from a variety of sources.

6.6 Encourage students to communicate their ideas through several modes.

6.7 Insure demonstration of acquisition of essential skills and concepts.

7. *Evaluation:* The evaluation of the specific TAG program will:

7.1 Be based on the goals and objectives delineated for each program.

7.2 Be used to modify the program whenever appropriate.

7.3 Take into account attitudes of students, teachers, and parents.

REASONS FOR DENIAL OF FUNDING

The following is a checklist for evaluators of program proposals for gifted and talented.* Although not all proposals follow the same guidelines, it would be valuable to be aware of what the readers of the proposals look for when considering them for funding.

_____The project did not demonstrate an innovative approach to the education of gifted and talented.

_____The project failed to show sufficient need for the proposed activities for the gifted and talented.

_____The objectives were not realistically attainable in relation to the identified needs of the gifted and talented.

_____The portion of project costs to be funded by the federal government is not reasonable in order to attain the expected benefits.

_____The background, training, and experience of the staff is not relevant to engaging in the education of the gifted and talented.

_____The project does not provide for periodic self-evaluation in such a manner as to influence the further thrust of the project.

_____The project is not cost effective in terms of federal investment.

_____The objectives were not specific and immediate in relation to the needs identified and did not contain *appropriate strategies* to meet these objectives.

_____The activities were not planned to meet the *unique needs of the individual.*

_____The activities did not incorporate *innovative concepts and techniques* which could be replanned to meet current problems expected in gifted and talented.

_____The project did not demonstrate expertise to train staff.

_____The project did not effectively and efficiently use existing monetary, human, and informational resources—public, private, and community.

_____The project did not demonstrate innovative coordination of resources for program management.

_____The program did not utilize objective assessment procedures.

---

*Adapted from "Reviewers' Comments," U.S.O.E./Gifted and Talented.

110

_____The evaluation plan did not directly or indirectly involve parents, students, or community in the evaluation process.

_____The evaluation plan did not *use* accomplishments of gifted *students* or their *teachers* as part of the evaluation process.

_____There were not sufficient monetary or human resources for organizing final results of the project in exportable form.

_____The in-service training is not comprehensive enough or of sufficient quality to make an impact.

_____The project does not demonstrate evidence of *substantial commitment or continuation* of training activities beyond funding period.

_____The project is not involving individuals who are *actively involved* with gifted and talented.

_____The project does not appear to have the scope *to effect a long-range and lasting change.*

_____The project does not utilize staff or consultants in such a manner as to *maximize resource management.*

_____The project is not part of a *comprehensive state plan* for individualizing and meeting special educational needs of gifted and talented.

_____The selection of the participants in the project does not indicate evidence of significant promise or commitment to the field of gifted.

_____The project does not provide *technical assistance and coordination services* for short-term interim training institutes at the *local level.*

_____The project does not plan to conduct periodic workshops on *topics of timely impact* to the gifted studies, culturally different, family relations, etc.

_____The project does not provide a *communication network* for leadership personnel.

_____The project does not adequately provide for the development of *training materials.*

_____The project does not provide short-term training of teams of leadership personnel from LEA's, private agencies, or institutions with a *wide national impact on education* of gifted and talented.

111

SAMPLE PROGRAMS

The following is a compilation of gifted and talented programs in operation throughout the country. These examples illustrate implementations of various program models to address many areas of giftedness. Since the intent is to stimulate ideas and suggest resources, we do not present these programs as "the best" but only as examples.

PACT: (Program for Academically and Creatively Talented)
Needham Public Schools
Needham, Massachusetts

GOAL

PACT focuses on the development of critical and creative thinking involving synthesis, analysis, and evaluation. The teaching of critical and creative thinking skills is basic to PACT classes because we recognize that PACT students, in particular, need to know how to ask and answer their own questions and how to make innovative and informed judgments and decisions.

Teaching for critical and creative thinking develops skills in students that will help them effectively analyze and evaluate information. Critical and creative thinking skills enable them to combine and transform ideas and information into new ways of thinking and acting.

OVERVIEW OF PACT

Students in grades 2–7 meet with a PACT teacher on a weekly basis with other PACT students at their grade level. Elementary students (grades 2–5) meet once a week for approximately two hours. Middle school students (grades 6–7) meet one period per week during the school day, with other optional school time arranged for special projects.

Grade 8 students are part of a special challenge project through the English/PACT curriculum in which the PACT activities are incorporated in the regular curriculum.

PACT AND THE REGULAR CURRICULUM

The inclusion of critical and creative thinking in the regular classroom is important. Resources are provided to teachers, and staff development planning and training is ongoing. Lessons by PACT teachers in the regular classroom have been initiated in order to integrate the teaching of critical and creative thinking into the regular curriculum.

112

IDENTIFICATION

Screening takes place in the spring and is based on requests by teachers and/or parents. Students are accepted into PACT on the basis of a combination of the following criteria:

1. Teacher Observations of class performance: Teacher Recommendation Forms and Renzulli Checklist

2. Achievement Scores

3. Torrance Test for Creativity: Selected sections

4. Slosson Intelligence Test Score: Test individually administered by a PACT instructor. Only children whose initial screening data are strong are tested.

Sample Pact Activity
Grade 8 English/PACT Program
Narrative Fiction Unit
Extended Enrichment Assignment

Skills: Researching, elaborating, collating data, making corrections, exploring different points of view, integrating and analyzing information.

When studying fiction one cannot help wondering about the craft of writing itself. How do writers get their ideas? Are all their ideas fully formed in advance of their writing? Where do they write? Do they use some special desk, in some special room? Do they need to be out in the country to write well? Some writers work best early in the morning. Others find their inspiration after midnight....

What follows is a THREE-PART assignment which centers around the art and act of writing. READ THROUGH CAREFULLY.

PART ONE:

Try to think about what and how you think when you do any writing. In a journal, start to record these thoughts. Include in your journals observations about the times of day when you have your most productive thoughts for writing. What particular place or places do you favor when you write? Are certain moods better for you than others? Do not be concerned with coming to any conclusions at this point. Concentrate on recording as many thoughts and ideas as you can.

PART TWO:

Talk to a writer. You may talk to a "famous" writer, or a parent, a friend, a relative, a journalist on a local newspaper—anyone who has any experience with writing. Part of this activity will be to develop a questionnaire for interviewing the writer. The types of questions you may want to ask are: (1) From where/what do you get your inspiration to write? (2) What "blocks" to writing do you experience? (3) Do you have a special place where you like to write? (4) When do you do most of your writing? (5) Why do you write? (6) How do you get started? and other questions you would develop.

INTERVIEW YOUR WRITER AND RECORD ALL YOUR INFORMATION.

PART THREE:

Find out what some well-known writers have said and written about their own writing. Many famous writers have written articles about how they think and how they proceed as they write.

MAKE NOTES WHEN YOU DO THIS RESEARCH.

You may record these notes in any way you wish and you will be encouraged to show these to the teacher.

FINAL EXERCISE: Compare and contrast the different responses and experiences people have when they are writing. What conclusions can you draw about the art and act of writing based on the comparisons you make? Can you make any generalizations about the processes of thinking that are behind the art of writing? What kinds of things have you learned about your own writing as a result of this investigation?

Project Prism at Foxborough
Foxborough Schools
Foxborough, Massachusetts 02035

Goal: To provide differentiated experiences appropriate for identified gifted and talented students in a variety of areas.

Identification Procedure: Teacher nomination, standardized tests, culture fair test.

Program Description: The program for gifted and talented students in Foxborough, grades 6–8, currently has three components:

1. Advanced experiences in visual and performing arts (band and art). Selected students participate in individual instructional sessions, and extracurricular activities such as ensembles and music festivals.

2. Minicourses. Selected students may engage in general courses such as "Futures" and "Alternative Energy Sources" which incorporate several academic disciplines. These courses are designed to accomplish several goals: (a) teach advanced skills and concepts; (b) engage students in high-level cognitive activities; and (c) encourage students to produce works reflective of their abilities.

3. Sponsored experiences. Individual or small groups of students may "contract" with teachers or mentors for projects in their own areas of interest. These contracts entail work at higher levels of cognition and require products reflecting the student's exceptional abilities.

The instruction and learning experiences in the minicourses and sponsored experiences are closely coordinated with classroom instruction so redundant and "extra" work for these students is minimized. In-service training is provided to help with coordination and implementation.

4. We are also considering a counseling component in which the selected students will focus on problems and conflicts unique to the gifted and talented.

Program Director: Role Description

1. Help students focus on areas of interest for "Prism Experiences." This is usually accomplished through personal interviews.

2. Help students and sponsors (mentors) formulate and describe the experience, ensuring continuity and differentiation.

3. Coordinate the student's work in the experience and his/her work in related classes to minimize redundancy and "extra" work.

4. Locate resources when necessary to facilitate the functioning of an experience.

5. Articulate the program to teachers and community.

6. Coordinate modification and expansion of the program.

7. Provide in-service training on meeting the needs of gifted and talented students.

Proposal for Experiences. When a student wishes to begin work in a particular area of interest, s/he and/or director locate a sponsor (mentor) and they develop an "Experience Proposal," describing the general program for the student. An example of a "Proposal for Experience" appears on page 117.

Individual Contract. Once the "Proposal for Experience" has been completed, the student meets with the sponsor (mentor) and completes an individual contract. Currently, the "Management Plan" developed by Joseph S. Renzulli provides the general format for the contract. An example of such a contract appears on pages 118–19.

After a student begins a "Prism Experience," the director sends a letter to the student's parents indicating with whom the student is working and stressing the commitment the student has accepted. An example of such a letter appears on page 120 and an accompanying description of the experience follows.

115

"Prism" Experience for Bill Maloney

Title of Experience: Book Review

Goal: To write a book review of a new book in the area of fantasy fiction.

Advanced Skills and Concepts Learned:
critical analysis of popular fiction, synthesis of information from several sources, development of criteria for evaluating books and writing book reviews for general consumption through the public libraries.

Description of Work Involved: Bill will read several books in the area of fantasy fiction and analyze them to determine what constitutes "good" fantasy fiction. At this point he will write a short essay citing the criteria he has established. Then Bill will read book reviews from several sources and determine the elements in a book review. After this he will be given a new fantasy fiction book and will write a book review about it. Then he will meet with other students and adults in the area to discuss and refine their book reviews. Finally, he will submit the finished book review for publication throughout the Boston area libraries.

Description of Final Product: The final product will be the published book review.

Proposal for Experience for G/T (Prism) Students

1. Goal of Experience: Produce and present a critical review of a literary work

2. Subject Area(s): LANGUAGE ARTS   (and subject areas related to nonfiction books)

3. Population: students from grades 6-8

   number 10

4. Selection Procedure: Self-selection, informal interview, teacher recommendation

5. Overview of Experience: Students will describe criteria for evaluating works in a particular area of interest. Students will read a fiction or nonfiction book and write a critical review. Some students will have the opportunity to present the review at a meeting. All accepted reviews will be published.

6. Basic skills and concepts covered through this experience: _____
   Reading   Writing (exposition)
   Speaking (presentations, discussion)

7. Advanced skills and concepts covered through this experience:
   Analysis   Critical thinking and evaluation
   Synthesis of information from several sources

8. Differentiation for Prism students (i.e., how is this different from what you would do with other students?) (1) Assuming ability to read fiction and nonfiction independently; (2) Discussions will begin at analysis level regarding literary works and essays; (3) Focus will be on establishing criteria for critical analysis; (4) Written book review will be for publication.

9. Resources needed: People Jane Shapiro, Fred Tuttle, Barbara Selvitella
   Materials Book Reviews   Novels   Other Transportation to libraries for book review discussions

10. Logistics: Time: TBA   Place: TBA

11. Evaluation: Students: Quality of reviews
    Experience: Discussion with students

117

MANAGEMENT PLAN FOR INDIVIDUA

NAME ___Bill Maloney___ GRADE ___7___

TEACHER ___Mr. Crowley___ SCHOOL ___Ahern___

GENERAL AREA(S) OF STUDY
(Check all that apply)

_x_ Language Arts/Humanities   __ Science   __ Personal and
Social Development

__ Social Studies   __ Music   __ Other (Specify)

__ Mathematics   __ Art   __ Other (Specify)

INTENDED AUDIENCES

Which individuals or groups would be most interested in the findings? List the organized groups (clubs, societies, teams) at the local, regional, state, and national levels. What are the names and addresses of contact persons in these groups? When and where do they meet?

1. ___Boston Public Libraries___

2. ___Teachers of English___

3. _____

4. _____

5. _____

INTENDED PRODUCT(S) AND OUTLETS

What form(s) will the final product take? How, when and where will you communicate the results of your investigation to an appropriate audience(s)? What outlet vehicles (journals, conferences, art shows, etc.) are typically used by professionals in this field?

1. Book review

2. List of criteria for evaluating fantasy fiction.

GETTING STARTED

What are the first steps you should take to begin this investigation? What types of information or data will be needed to solve the problem? If "raw data," how can it be gathered, classified, and presented? If you plan to use already categorized information or data, where is it located and how can you obtain what you need?

Read fantasy fiction books and critical essays and discuss with others.

ND SMALL GROUP INVESTIGATIONS

Beginning Date __10/1__   **Estimated Ending Date** __12/4__

Progress Reports Due on Following Dates __10/22__   __11/4__   __11/25__

SPECIFIC AREA OF STUDY
Write a brief description of the problem that you plan to investigate. What are the objectives of your investigation? What do you hope to find out?

What are the elements that distinguish fantasy fiction from other modes?
Objective: Write a critical review of a fantasy fiction novel.

METHODOLOGICAL RESOURCES AND ACTIVITIES
List the names and addresses of persons who might provide assistance in attacking this problem. List the how-to-do-it books that are available in this area of study. List other resources (films, collections, exhibits, etc.) and special equipment (e.g., camera, transit, tape recorder, questionnaire, etc.). Keep a continuous record of all activities that are part of this investigation.

Resources: 1. People – Dr. Tuttle – Ahern School
                 – Mr. Crowley – Ahern School
                 – Mrs. Selvitella – High School
                 – father – home

         2. Readings –
                 – Fantasy fiction books (see back for list)
                 – Critical essays on fantasy fiction
                 – Book Reviews

Steps: 1. Read fantasy fiction books
            2. Read critical essays
            3. Discuss elements of fantasy fiction with sponsor and/or resource people
            4. Write list of evaluation criteria for fantasy fiction
            5. Read and discuss various book reviews
            6. Write draft of book review for new fantasy fiction novel
            7. Share draft with others
            8. Revise book review and submit for publication

From *A Guidebook for Developing Individualized Educational Programs for Gifted and Talented Students* (page 38, actual size: 11x17) by Joseph S. Renzulli and Linda H. Smith (Mansfield Center, Conn.: Creative Learning Press, 1979).

Sample Letter to Parents

Dear Mr. and Mrs. Maloney:

Bill has made arrangements to work with Mr. Crowley, a teacher of English at the Ahern Intermediate School, to participate in the attached "Prism" experience. This experience represents a commitment in time and effort for both Bill and Mr. Crowley. Although we will try to coordinate some of this work with his regular classroom work, I am sure Bill will spend some extra time with it.

Following completion of the review, Bill will receive recognition of his efforts by having it published and circulated among several Boston area public libraries and some arrangements will be made for academic recognition through his English class.

If you have any questions about this or the program in general, please contact me.

Sincerely,

Frederick B. Tuttle, Jr.
Director: Program for
Gifted and Talented

Sample Primary Investigation: Renzulli

Prototype of a Type III Enrichment Activity in Social Science*

A small group of students in a middle-grade program for the academically talented got into an argument about an issue over which political candidates were divided in a forthcoming election for city government. The issue involved the construction of an oil refinery on the city's waterfront and opinion was divided over whether or not the majority of voters were in favor of the project. Some students supported the position of candidates who were against the refinery because of environmental concerns while others felt that the refinery was needed to help the city's sagging economy and high unemployment rate.

The students decided that they would like to assess the status of voters' attitudes and the teacher helped to focus the problem by suggesting that the students conduct a questionnaire study. It was at this crucial point that the teacher decided to provide the youngsters with methodological assistance only, and to do this she consulted with a librarian at a nearby college. The librarian suggested that the teacher look through the sections on Psychometrics and Questionnaires and she quickly located the following books:

Oppenheim, A. N. *Questionnaire Design and Attitude Measurement.* New York: Basic Books, 1966, 298 pp.

Shaw, M. & Wright J. *Scales for the Measurement of Attitudes.* New York: McGraw-Hill, 1967, 372 pp.

These books deal with basic issues in the methodology of attitude study such as instrument design, question wording, sampling, and advantages and disadvantages of several scaling techniques. The book by Shaw and Wright also included a compendium of various types of questionnaires, checklists, and rating scales. The teacher also brought in a few sample copies of a journal that she located entitled *Public Opinion Quarterly* and this helped to heighten student interest about the entire field of polling and attitude measurement. Although these materials are written for college-level students, the gifted youngsters were able to understand most of them and the teacher assisted by explaining some of the more difficult concepts. Following suggestions outlined in Oppenheim's book, the youngsters constructed a pilot version of their questionnaire and field tested it on a small sample of students and parents. Feedback obtained from field testing was used to revise certain aspects of the instructions and a number of items after which a final version of the questionnaire was mailed to a random sample of citizens in the community. The teacher provided additional methodological assistance by obtaining the following two books:

Blalock, Hubert. *Social Statistics.* New York: McGraw-Hill, 1960, 465 pp.

---

*From *The Enrichment Triad Model* by Joseph Renzulli (Mansfield Center, Conn.: Creative Learning Press, 1977).

Smith, G. Milton. *A Simplified Guide to Statistics,* (4th ed.) New York: Holt, Rinehart, and Winston, 1962, 244 pp.

These books contain discussions about how to analyze types of data obtained from questionnaires and they also include information about how to prepare histograms and graphic representations of statistical findings. The students developed statistical, narrative and graphic summaries of the results of their investigation and prepared a final report. Presentations about the results of the study were made to other groups of students and to persons attending a PTA meeting. Parts of the report were also included in a newsletter distributed by the school and in the school news section of a local newspaper.

The following program descriptions (Project Pegasus, Acres of Diamonds Talented and Gifted Program, Advanced Programs of Palo Alto, Project Potential, Identification and Programs for TAG Oriented Students, and K–12 Programming for Gifted Students) are from Joyce Juntune's book (J).*

PROJECT PEGASUS
Child Development Department
Iowa State University
Ames, Iowa 50011
(515) 294–4111

LEVELS: 3–5-year-old students (nursery school)

PROGRAM DESCRIPTION

A model nursery school gifted program for 18 students, ages 3–5, based on Renzulli's Enrichment Triad Model. Includes curriculum and parent education materials, teacher training, and community resource coordination. Laboratory classroom setting at Iowa State University, Child Development Department.

IDENTIFICATION

Parent Nomination; Renzulli/Hartman-Behavioral Characteristics of Superior Students; Stanford-Binet, Form L-M, 1972 Norms; Torrance: Thinking Creatively in Action and Movement; Illinois Test of Psycholinguistic Ability

EVALUATION MEASURES USED

A variety of standardized tests will be used along with a questionnaire filled out by parents, teachers, and student participants. Independent judge evaluation will be collected every 2 months. Finally, parent/teacher conferences will include an evaluation component.

VISITATION INFORMATION

Visitors are welcome. Contact: Dr. Dianne Draper, Director, Ms. Martha Jacobson, Head Teacher. Mondays–Fridays, 2:00–4:30 p.m.

Iowa currently has no nursery school programs exclusively for the gifted. To begin to serve this neglected population, Project Pegasus will become part of the 57-year-old early education program in the Child Development

*Successful Programs for the Gifted and Talented, edited by Joyce Juntune (St. Paul: National Association for Gifted Children, 1981). Reprinted with permission.

123

Department at Iowa State University for the 1981-83 school year. This setting will provide: exposure of the curriculum to a wide audience, training opportunities for students and educators, and a strong research base for evaluation of programming efforts.

Project Pegasus will be primarily based on Renzulli's Enrichment Triad Model. The goal of Project Pegasus is to develop and implement a model program for gifted and talented preschoolers that will:

- nurture their special abilities
- include a parent involvement component
- attempt to coordinate relevant community resources for these preschoolers and their families
- make available to others the products of this program (e.g., curriculum and parent education materials).

Project Pegasus will provide a range of learning experiences for the students designed to encourage the development of:

- thinking skills, such as analyzing, synthesizing and critical evaluating
- curiosity and the ability to create new ideas and originate new lines of thought
- task commitment, increased attention span, and persistence in the application of thought
- communication skills, such as expressional and associational fluency as well as reading
- abilities related to planning, organizing, adapting, and decision making
- skills to enhance his/her ability to cope with the social/educational mainstream
- individual talents in depth and breadth.

Special objectives of the parent component include provision of:

- a responsive environment in which they can discuss their concerns, joys, problems, and successes with their gifted child in order to strengthen their family relationship
- information on the principles of educating gifted children as well as activities related to their child's program which could be implemented outside the classroom.

Project Pegasus will serve as an educational opportunity for students and faculty to work with gifted children for the purposes of:

- training child development students and student teachers
- serving as a model for the development, implementation, and evaluation of appropriate gifted and talented preschool curricula

124

- having outside observers learn from our efforts.

The final objective is for the project staff to serve as a liaison between the home, school, and community in order to coordinate available resources for the gifted.

Funding for Project Pegasus is provided by the Northwest Area Foundation. The funding period covers two years. The first year, 1980–81, includes the following activities:

- to develop curriculum and parent resource material
- to identify target students
- to train in-service staff
- to plan and begin liaison efforts.

The second year, 1981-82, includes:

- implementation of program and evaluation
- continuation of in-service development
- continuation of liaison efforts.

Students will be screened for intellectual and academic ability, creativity, and task commitment. Parent and teacher nominations will also be considered. From the screening pool, 9 boys and 9 girls with the highest scores on the screening battery will be selected for the program.

Evaluation of students will be done in September and May of the 1981–82 school year. Teacher evaluation of each student will be done biannually. Two judges, who are independent of the project, will observe the program every two months to rate its effectiveness. Biweekly curriculum evaluations will be made by the teaching staff.

ACRES OF DIAMONDS TALENTED AND GIFTED PROGRAM
Portage Township Schools
5894 Central Avenue
Portage, Indiana 46368
(219) 762-6511, ext. 333 or 206

LEVELS: Grades K–5. The program concepts are appropriate for K–12.

PROGRAM DESCRIPTION

The Acres of Diamonds program seeks to identify a wide range of areas of potential within as many students as possible and to provide for the development of this potential through specific teaching/learning strategies, materials, and community resources. High-level thinking skills are developed through five talent areas: Creative Thinking, Forecasting, Communicating, Planning, and Decision Making.

Any or all major program components could be adopted or adapted:

1. General Classroom Activities—a variety of activities threaded into the regular curriculum to develop the five talent areas.

2. Challenge Centers—learning centers designed by the classroom teacher which specifically develop high-level thought processes through the five talent areas.

3. Independent Study Projects—individual or small groups of students participate in actual research, so they think, act, and feel as the practicing professional.

4. Creative Writing Program—small groups of students identified as having creative writing potential meet outside the regular classroom to develop their talent.

The program rationale is based on the multiple talent research of Dr. Calvin Taylor, which urges the breaking away from a narrow educational emphasis on academic talents and stresses the development of a broad spectrum of high-level thought processes. Development of various program components also draws upon the works of J. P. Guilford, Sidney J. Parnes, Joseph Renzulli, E. Paul Torrance, and Frank Williams.

The program is one which can be implemented at all grade levels in any area of the curriculum with individuals, small groups, or an entire class. This program meets the urgent and growing need for the development of a broad range of intellectual areas (many of which are not identified through tests or academic performance) to enable students to deal effectively with their personal needs as well as the complex challenges of our future society. Teachers are also encouraged to recognize their own strengths and talents and utilize these within the program.

Further programming during the 1980–81 school year at the middle school levels will build upon the five talent areas while broadening out into the areas of visual arts and problem-solving skills.

IDENTIFICATION

Teacher recommendation forms, Creative Writing Talent/Identification Activities, Student Interest Surveys, Performance in TAG (Talented and Gifted) activities, cumulative records.

EVALUATION MEASURES USED

Piers Harris Children's Self-Concept Scale, Torrance Tests of Creative Thinking, program evaluation by teachers (locally devised), program evaluation by students (locally devised).

EVALUATION RESULTS

Results indicated an increase in self-concept and creativity between a pre/post period during a three-year period.

MATERIALS AVAILABLE

Bibliography of Resources for the Talented and Gifted, "Everything You've Wanted to Know About Challenge Centers"—$3.00 each; "A Box of Gems from the Acres of Diamonds Talented and Gifted Program"—$15.00 each; "Planning Guide for Talented and Gifted Activities"—$2.00 each.

VISITATION INFORMATION

Visitors are welcome on Wednesdays and Thursdays. Contact Dr. Imogene Jones (Director) or Mrs. Marjorie Lewan (Coordinator)—(219) 762–6511, ext. 206 or 333 to make arrangements.

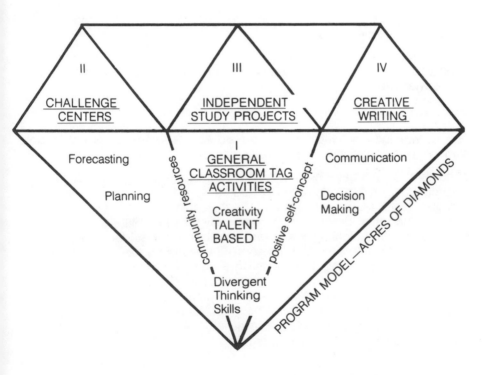

ADVANCED PROGRAMS
25 Churchill Avenue
Palo Alto, California 94306
(415) 855-8267

LEVELS: Grades K-12

PROGRAM DESCRIPTION

The project consists of Enrichment Classes, Resource Specialists, Independent Study Center, Alternative High School, Honors, and Advanced Placement.

IDENTIFICATION

Teacher judgment, individual assessments, and some group measures.

EVALUATION MEASURES USED

District-designed instruments to measure parent satisfaction, student satisfaction, and teacher satisfaction.

"Our willingness to expect from each other and to give full measure in return, our willingness to seek the truth and be guided by our findings, and our eternal drive to improve on what we are doing, have fostered a qualitative education for which we need make no apologies." (Robert E. Shutes, Palo Alto Unified School District, 1963)

And so was the spirit with which the Palo Alto program for especially able students was conceived. And so has it continued.

A combination of genetics, environment, and exemplary instruction have resulted in a unique population of students in Palo Alto. The city which harbors Stanford University has a student population of 10,500, 20 percent of whom are either identified as academically gifted by State or local criteria, or who act gifted. Among this gifted population are students identified as highly gifted: that is, students who score 3+ standard deviations above the mean on individual intelligence tests. In a normal distribution such students number 13 in 10,000; in Palo Alto they number 493. Clearly high aptitude is a significant characteristic of the student population. Consequently, program planning for the special needs of the population has traditionally been expected by the community and delivered with pleasure by those staff members who work with the gifted student.

Not all staff members enjoy working with gifted students. We recognize that careful selection of teachers who work closely with all students is essential. Additionally appropriate, however, is the careful selection of teachers who work with the especially able.

When some gifted students were asked in a study completed not long ago,

128

"With what kind of teacher do you learn best, most enjoyably and in depth?" responses included "... a teacher that lets you do independent work"... "a teacher who lets you work at your own speed "... "a teacher who gives you a choice—I like to discover facts and things rather than having someone tell me"... "I like a teacher who does not help you all the time, only when you really need it"... "a teacher who acts like he really cares for you and makes things fun for the whole class"... "one who does not interrupt and change the subject"... "a teacher who takes suggestions"... "a teacher who is humorous and playful in his approach to instruction."

Gifted students can be difficult for teachers. On October 31, 1975, Charles McCable, popular columnist in the San Francisco *Chronicle*, spoke of the traits of the gifted student:

> Gifted kids are "high spirited" if you like them, "emotionally unstable" if you don't. If he lets his feelings rip, the gifted child is urged by his teacher to pipe down or more commonly nowadays he is placed on a regimen of retalin or some other kind of drug which, among other bad effects, interferes with the play of his feelings which is the gifted child's capital. This kind of child can be told two things: that he is showing independence and that he is admirable or that he is being rebellious and, therefore, bad. There is nothing of malice in the gifted child's asserting of highly individual self. When his independence is seen to be malicious, the fight for the gifted child and what he can offer society is just about lost.

In response to the kind of students with whom we are working, in recognition of the need for careful instruction, and in recognition of the kinds of environment in which students learn best, we proceeded to develop a program.

Prior to July 1, 1980, the State of California provided financial support for students who met its criteria for intellectually gifted—the state program was called MGM—Mentally Gifted Minor.

Since July 1, 1980, the definition of gifted was broadened from only the intellectually gifted to include those gifted in leadership, creativity, special academic areas, visual and performing arts, and students who perform at a high achievement level. It is now called Gifted and Talented. Palo Alto elected to continue to serve the large academically talented population but also to embrace the high achiever and to provide some special assistance in some specific academic areas.

Accommodations for the gifted and talented at the elementary level occur basically within the self-contained, heterogeneously grouped classrooms. Within a school that uses teaming or is nongrade, provisions for able students become a part of that structure.

We have not elected to segregate elementary-school-age gifted students into special day classes as is often done because:

- Able youngsters exist in every school and at every level in our district; they consequently form an instructional group in most classrooms.
- Our responsibility to these students does not rest only in the academic skill areas, but includes providing opportunities to interact, play, learn, and problem solve with students representing all backgrounds and ability levels.

Instructional planning for the youngster or groups of youngsters who learn rapidly and easily within each school occurs as a part of the planning for all students. That is, we must be sensitive and responsive to the uniqueness of each student, the able student among them. This student must not be left to learn on his own—get along. We cannot assume he will get along anyway. Skillful teaching is essential if he is to reach his potential.

Provisions typically take the form of enrichment, or—as the state mandates—"qualitative difference." Something must be different about the G/T curriculum—not more of the same, such as ten book reports instead of five, or twenty math problems instead of ten, or a research paper of ninety pages instead of five. Instead, a teacher must deliberately differentiate the program content and activities from that which is typically taught.

Examples of Palo Alto enrichment can be found in our literature, math, science, and social studies programs, most of which were developed by the district. The Enrichment Readers, for instance, are a collection of 38 books, each of which is accompanied by a study guide which leads students to consider notions which would not necessarily be available to them in the course of their regular school experience. The books are selected on the basis of interest to students and complexity of concept. An example of literature enrichment is the story *Wind in the Willows*, which we teach to very able readers in grade four. In the story, Toad says, among many other things, "Live for others, that's my motto in life." The students were asked if Toad is serious in this declaration. What effect does it have on the reader? What do later events tell us about Toad? Or, the suggestion is made to ask students to write on: "Mole as a student in my classroom," or "Badger as a Palo Alto businessman," or "A Modern Wildwood," or "The Principal's Name is Badger." Other titles include *Robin Hood, Amos Fortune, Free Man, Phantom Tollbooth, San Francisco Bay, Sea Around Us, Kon-Tiki.*

Able math students are expected to develop depth and breadth within the regular math curriculum at each grade level by expanding and extending their understandings. Special materials and resources are available for this purpose. Acceleration in math may also occur when a student has mastered the concepts for the grade and has experienced the enrichment program. However, factors indicating real ability are considered before such acceleration occurs.

Our social studies and science curricula contain specific activities and opportunities for allowing the especially able/interested student to achieve greater satisfaction from a topic.

Providing individualized programs for able youngsters is difficult in the regular classroom. In recognition of this difficulty, we employ two teacher specialists who help classroom teachers plan instructional programs for gifted students. Their role is consultant, expeditor, facilitator. We surveyed the staff recently to discover if the resource teachers were responding to the needs of classroom teachers. We received an 85 percent response: Nearly 80 percent of the classroom teachers said that they were able to work with gifted students "much better" or "somewhat better" as a result of the involvement of resource teachers.

There are two middle schools in the PAUSD and two different systems of providing programs for the gifted. Common among these are Honors classes in greater or lesser numbers. An Honors class must distinguish itself from the "regular" curriculum in breadth and most especially depth of instruction. It may employ a text for a higher level, deeper exploration of a topic, special projects which may not be related to the curriculum for the grade, and/or more emphasis on an experience in creativity. As in gifted programs in the elementary schools, a higher level of cognition characterizes Honors classes. Middle School A, with a gifted population of 202 out of 760, has a full-blown Honors program in all subject areas into which the able youngsters are scheduled. Middle School B, with 238 gifted students in a school of 831, offers a mix of programs: they have Honors classes; they have heterogeneous groupings. They also have a vertical team, which allows the students to move through the middle school curriculum at their own rate, and a horizontal team, which holds students in a pattern of enrichment instead of moving them ahead. One element of Middle School B is a program referred to affectionately as the "Intellectual Pool Hall." This Pool Hall is designed to supplement educational opportunities for the student with high ability and achievement potential. In more prosaic terms, it is called the Independent Study Center. It allows qualified students to be released from a class one day or more a week with teacher approval in order to pursue subjects of high interest to them. Most instruction in the Independent Study Center takes place in group seminars. One such seminar is called "Life Lines." The students explore the patterns of people's lives from childhood through schooling, career and old age. They ask: what were the important decisions in these lives, how were they made, what part does chance or intent play, or character or talent? Do people continue to change as they grow older? A seminar in mythology is where the students are reading Greek or Roman myths and creating board games using information from their readings. An example might be, you land on the sphinx square and you must answer a question. If you fail, you go to Hades and miss two turns. French conversation, German conversation, Chess, Great Books Seminars are other topics. Recently an IMSAI computer added some pizzazz to the Pool Hall.

Having saluted autonomy and individualization in the elementary and middle schools, we recognized the need for more rigor, preparation for college, GPA's, PSAT's and SAT's in our two high schools. This recognition led to a

131

fairly consistent pattern of Honors and Advanced Placement classes.

The Advanced Placement program is a cooperative venture between secondary schools and colleges throughout the United States to meet the special needs of very able students. In Palo Alto, the term is applied to a sequence of courses which lead to college level work in the high school, usually at the twelfth grade, though students may elect to take AP classes at whatever point in high school that their preparation is completed. The program enables students to progress at a faster rate, to avoid duplicating superior high school work at the college level, and to save some time and money in a college program heavily loaded with required subjects. When the sequence has been completed successfully, students are strongly encouraged to take special placement examinations prepared by the College Entrance Examination Board and submit the results to their chosen college with a request for advanced placement in the subject area of the examination.

Our efforts have not been in vain. In 1976, 529 high school students took 559 advanced placement exams: 346 achieved High Honors and Honors. In 1977, 425 exams were taken by 294 students, and 275 achieved High Honors and Honors. Of the 35 National Merit semifinalists in 1977 from Palo Alto, 33 were finalists and six received scholarship awards. In 1978, we had 46 semifinalists, 44 went on to be finalists and 11 received scholarship awards. Of the 340 students who took 662 exams in 1978, 224 achieved High Honors and Honors. There were 32 National Merit finalists in 1978 and 36 in 1979. 1979 AP Exam results showed that 249 of the 380 students taking the exam achieved High Honors and Honors.

Most colleges in the United States grant advanced placement to students who do well on the Advanced Placement Examination; some colleges also grant college credit for a freshman level course given in the senior year of high school. Students may thus save a year's time in that subject in college. Student evaluations of the program in Palo Alto tell us. "Take away what you will, but leave us our Honors and AP classes."

In conclusion, let me say that we have some worries. We worry about the time to complete the task as it should be done. We worry about the wisest use of available money. Most of all, we worry about the attitude which continues to exist in some communities that it is inappropriate to expend resources for this group of students with exceptional needs, students who have the potential to participate in solving the ever increasingly complex problems of mankind. Our responsibility is to help each one of them achieve a wholesome, effective marriage of heart and mind.

Ruthe A. Lundy
Coordinator, Elementary Education and
Advanced Programs Departments

PROJECT POTENTIAL
Washington Elementary School District
8610 North 19th Avenue
Phoenix, Arizona 85021
(602) 995-6164

LEVELS: Grades K-8

PROGRAM DESCRIPTION

We have a resource room for gifted students in each of our 31 schools. Because we serve about 1300 students, which is approximately 5 percent of our total school population, the resource room teachers are not able to serve all the students. Therefore we also have 20 enrichment components done by regular classroom teachers, and some extended programs on Saturdays, weekends and summer.

IDENTIFICATION

The State of Arizona is in the process of determining an achievement test to be used for placement of the gifted students. Our district uses multiple criteria. We use the Wechsler Intelligence Scale-R, Achievement tests and teacher and parent recommendation. We also have a district chorus. Students are identified by community experts and the chorus teacher.

EVALUATION MEASURES USED

We use pre- and post-tests in the academic areas. We use observation scales developed by the pupils and teachers at the beginning of each year. We also send surveys out to parents and regular classroom teachers each year.

EVALUATION RESULTS

So far our students, parents and teachers have been very favorable toward our program. We have been in existence for seven years. As our program has developed from a small and not very sophisticated one to a broad-scoped and individualized program, the entire school community feels that the level of learning in each class is up in part because of the program.

MATERIALS AVAILABLE

1. Project Potential Handbook. This is 125 pages and we will send it for the price of the postage. At this time the postage has not been determined.

2. Scope and Sequence. This document gives the philosophy, goals, and objectives of Project Potential. It gives a broad outline of the material taught in the total program, and the sequence in which it is taught. Send postage.

VISITATION INFORMATION

Visitors are welcome if arrangements are made in advance. Phone or write Bobbie Kraver, 8610 North 19th Avenue, Phoenix, Arizona 85021 (602) 995-6164.

Project Potential is Washington School District's program for Gifted and Talented Students. It is an extensive and carefully planned program designed to provide unique educational opportunities. The goal of Project Potential is to provide an environment that allows students to interact with other students who can challenge them on their intellectual level.

The school district has approximately 15,000 students in 31 schools. It is located in a middle- to upper-middle-class area of Phoenix, Arizona. It is an elementary district of Kindergarten through grade 8.

We have the equivalent of 23 full-time teachers. By that I mean that 21 teachers are full time and 4 teachers have asked to teach half time. In addition to that, we have 20 regular classroom teachers who work with gifted students during designated school periods, and about 30 volunteer parents who help with Super Saturday programs and help to organize and run a four-week summer school program. Included in the 23 teachers is one man who works totally with choral music.

Our students are identified by multiple criteria. We use achievement test scores. This is in keeping with the new mandate passed by the State of Arizona which states that students who score two standard deviations above the norm on a test to be determined by the State will qualify for special academic programs. In addition to this, our district also uses IQs, and/or creative productive performance. For those students in the music program, identification is made by the choral music teacher with assistance from experts in the community.

Evaluation of our programs has been based on parent, teacher, and student surveys taken at the end of each school year, and pre- and post-test scores in the academic areas.

It is our goal to provide excellent programs for all gifted students in our school district. As in all school districts, there just is not enough money to fulfill that goal. The thrust, therefore, will be to train every classroom in the Washington School District to know the characteristics of gifted students. We will then have in-service training available throughout the year for all teachers who want to work with the gifted students in the regular classroom. Our resource room teachers and trained community volunteers also go into the regular classroom to provide activities for the bright and gifted students.

In an effort to save money we also try to provide excellent training for our teachers by sharing consultants and in-service with neighboring districts. The Washington Elementary District's Project Potential Program is considered to be one of the finest in Arizona and we are trying to improve each year.

IDENTIFICATION AND PROGRAMS FOR TAG ORIENTED STUDENTS
(A working model at the Des Moines Art Center)
Greenwood Park
Des Moines, Iowa 50312
(515) 277-4405

LEVELS: Grades 4 and 5

PROGRAM DESCRIPTION

The purpose of this project is to provide area elementary schools with a program by which fourth and fifth grade students, exhibiting superior interest and ability, can learn, explore, understand, and create in the visual arts.

IDENTIFICATION

The students are identified through the use of the Burbank Visual Literacy Test. This is a specifically designed instrument used to identify visually talented and gifted students.

EVALUATION MEASURES USED

Two-part format: (1) twice a year both students and teachers will be asked to fill out Evaluation Sheets, (2) at the end of the year a cumulative student work show for parents, teachers, and project administrators will be held.

EVALUATION RESULTS

Project is in progress so we only have the first set of student-teacher evaluations. We have 100 percent positive feedback to this date.

MATERIALS AVAILABLE

The Burbank Visual Literacy Test is available on a consultant basis only.

VISITATION INFORMATION

Visitors welcome by appointment. Call the Des Moines Art Center Education Department (515) 277-4405. All TAG classes take place on Saturdays from 1:00-3:00.

The Des Moines Art Center, otherwise known as the Edmundson Art Foundation, is a private, nonprofit museum in Iowa's capital city. An internationally known art museum with a unique art collection, it also incorporates a complete art school. The Education Department of the DMAC, in conjunction with two local school districts, has fostered a general scholarship program for young people 9 through 18 since 1974. This highly successful program, based mainly on need rather than ability, was initiated and entirely supported financially by the DMAC for many years prior to the participation with the school districts. Because of the identified need for TAG programs in the past few years, the DMAC proposes to meet this challenge with a unique scholarship program for gifted and talented students.

The purpose of this project is to provide the Des Moines public and parochial elementary schools a program by which fourth and fifth grade students, exhibiting superior interest and ability, can learn, explore, understand, and create in the visual arts. The main focus of this program is to identify and select talented and gifted students, provide a wide range of visual arts programs, and help each student obtain the necessary educational tools to fulfill creative desires and develop aesthetic senses. This program will take place throughout the school year at the Des Moines Art Center.

The main focus of this program is to accomplish the following: (1) Identify and select talented and gifted students who exhibit both interest and ability in the visual arts. (2) Provide a wide range of programs which cover a cross-section of topics in art and give each child the opportunity to cover four subject areas with a broad range of creative experiences. (3) Help each student obtain the necessary educational tools for fulfilling his creative senses.

The population to be served is the Greater Des Moines public and parochial elementary schools (49 public schools and 12 parochial schools) specifically focusing on the fourth and fifth grade students. Each school within said category would be awarded two scholarships each year, one for a fourth grade student and one for a fifth grade student.

Evaluation of the program will have a two-part format. This format covers the stated objective, for at the conclusion of this program each student will have had an exposure to a variety of art classes which will enable him to have command of the visual arts. The evaluation format will be as follows: (1) twice each year (December and May) both student and teacher will be asked to fill out an evaluation sheet. These forms will be read and further evaluated by the education staff at the Des Moines Art Center and kept on file for reference. (2) at the end of the school year teachers will be asked to submit student work which shows exceptional ability. This work will then be hung in an Art Center school wing exhibition honoring TAG students in these classes. There will be a reception for the opening of this show where parents and teachers will be invited to view the art work of the TAG scholarship students. This show in itself will act as an evaluation, for only exceptional work will be selected and hung in the Des Moines Art Center Talented and Gifted exhibition.

K-12 PROGRAMMING FOR GIFTED STUDENTS
St. Louis Park Schools
6425 West 33rd Street
St Louis Park, Minnesota 55426
(612) 925-4300, ext. 238

LEVELS: Grades K-12

PROGRAM DESCRIPTION

The K-12 program includes a variety of options. The elementary program centers around enrichment activities by the classroom teacher. Special course offerings and acceleration are available to secondary students.

IDENTIFICATION

Achievement and aptitude as measured by standardized test scores; grades and/or performance; checklists of characteristics; judgments of teachers and other qualified personnel.

EVALUATION MEASURES USED

Program evaluation has been accomplished mainly through consumer evaluation questionnaires and conferences with teachers (regular classroom and gifted education), students and parents. Periodic reports are written about the progress of gifted students in the special classes.

EVALUATION RESULTS

The results from the informal and consumer evaluations indicate a positive and growth-producing impact on gifted students.

VISITATION INFORMATION

Visitors welcome by appointment. Contact Donna J. McBrian, K-12 Gifted Education Coordinator/Consultant, if further information or a visitation date is desired.

Philosophy

The District recognizes gifted and talented students as an integral part of the school system. Yet we understand that high potential students have learning styles and thinking dimensions which demand enrichment experiences beyond the basic curriculum. In recent years, the school system has sought to increase the opportunities for high potential students by introducing special curricula, providing enrichment and offering accelerated and special classes. Whenever appropriate, these programs are placed within the mainstream which will encourage lifelong learning, optimum development of particular gifts and talents, and development of leadership.

Components

The gifted program in St. Louis Park contains many components. Among them are—

1. Continuing in-service for total staff on Gifted-Awareness/New Strategies for Meeting Needs/Curriculum Development.

2. Gifted Education Resource Center—resource materials are available here for teachers, students, and parents.

3. Early admission to school

4. Acceleration

   a. content
   b. grade "skipping"

5. Enrichment via the regular classroom teacher through curriculum modification and independent study

6. Summer school program—a five-district consortium program for gifted students grades 4–12

7. Advanced Placement Courses

8. Concurrent registration with University

9. Early graduation

10. Periodic seminars for students Grades 4–12

11. Community sponsor/mentors/volunteer programs

12. Independent Study

13. "Pullout" class opportunities

    a. *K–Three Itinerant Teacher Program*

    The curriculum being used is designed around a thematic approach and includes several disciplines. It emphasizes higher-level thinking skills, and creative problem-finding and -solving skills. The program is meant to be a component of total programming efforts and a complement to what has been planned for the gifted student by a regular classroom teacher.

    The class meets twice a week for approximately 2½ hours—a total of five hours.

    b. *Four–Six Program*

    In grades four–six special classes for gifted are being taught by regular classroom teachers who are released for this purpose. The classes meet once a week for approximately 2½ hours. Five six-week

138

units are explored during the course of the year. Some of the courses offered this year:

- *Stocks and Stuff*
- *Solar Energy and Other Energy Alternatives*
- *Video Taping with a Focus on Children's Literature*
- *The M and M Year—Living in the Year 2000 and Beyond*
- *Photography Projects or Picture Power*
- *Note It, Kids!—Development of Research Skills*
- *Differences of Opinion*
- *Oceanography*
- *Creative Writing*
- *The Artist and His/Her Imagination.*

These classes will also emphasize higher-level thinking skills and the creative processes.

c. *Pro-Active Counselor Program for Gifted Secondary Students (7–12)*

The counselor actively seeks out students for individual and small group sessions on issues of concern to them. He also designs sessions to develop problem-finding and -solving skills, research skills, listening skills, and confrontive skills, and to explore the scope and breadth of opportunities available through the Career Center, community resources, and field trips; as well as act as an independent study facilitator. The goals for the year follow:

(1) To help gifted students explore their feelings and concerns. (Where they are now and to set goals and directions for the future)

(2) To create open, honest communication in small groups with peers. (Including skills of active listening and creative problem solving)

(3) To improve the self-concept of each member and acceptance of each for his/her uniqueness.

(4) To help gifted students clarify their values and assess their own strengths and needs.

(5) To help gifted students explore career opportunities which will be congruent with their lifestyle.

(6) To help gifted students become aware of their individual and societal contributions and responsibilities.

(7) To implement and develop pragmatic experiences at the three levels as appropriate (7 and 8), (9 and 10), (11 and 12).

SELECTED REFERENCES

Books and Articles

Abraham, W. *Common Sense About Gifted Children.* New York: Harper and Bros., 1958.

Adams, James L. *Conceptual Blockbusting: A Pleasurable Guide to Better Problem Solving.* New York: W. W. Norton and Co., 1974.

Assagioli, Roberto. "The Education of Gifted and Super-Gifted Children." New York: Psychosynthesis Foundation, 1960.

Bishop, W. E. "Characteristics of Teachers Judged Successful by Intellectually Gifted, High-Achieving High School Students." In W. B. Barbe and J. S. Renzulli, eds., *Psychology and Education of the Gifted.* 2d ed. New York: Irvington Publishers, 1975.

Bloom, B. S. ed. *Taxonomy of Educational Objectives. Handbook 1: Cognitive Domain.* New York: David McKay, 1956.

Boston, Bruce O. *A. Resource Manual of Information on Educating the Gifted and Talented.* Reston, Va.: Council for Exceptional Children, 1975.

——. *The Sorcerer's Apprentice: A Case Study in the Role of the Mentor.* Reston, Va.: Council for Exceptional Children, 1976.

——, ed. *Gifted and Talented: Developing Elementary and Secondary School Programs.* Reston, Va.: Council for Exceptional Children, 1975.

Callahan, Carolyn M. *Developing Creativity in the Gifted and Talented.* Reston, Va.: Council for Exceptional Children, 1978.

Clark, Barbara. *Growing Up Gifted.* Columbus, Ohio: Merrill, 1983.

DeBono, Edward. *Children Solve Problems.* New York: Harper and Row, 1974.

DeHaan, R., and Havighurst, R. J. *Educating Gifted Children.* Chicago: University of Chicago Press, 1957.

Feldhusen, J., and Treffinger, D. *Teaching Creative Thinking and Problem Solving.* Dubuque, Iowa: Kendall-Hunt Publishing Co., 1976.

Gallagher, J. J. *Teaching the Gifted Child.* Boston: Allyn and Bacon, 1975.

——. *Research Summary on Gifted Child Education.* Springfield, Ill.:

Office of the Superintendent of Public Instruction, 1966.

Gallagher, J. J.; Ashner, Mary Jane; and Jenne, William. *Productive Thinking of Gifted Children in Classroom Interaction.* Reston, Va.: Council for Exceptional Children, 1967.

Gartner, Alan, and Riessman, Frank. *How to Individualize Learning.* Bloomington, Ind.: Phi Delta Kappa Educational Foundation, 1977.

Ginsberg, Gina, and Harrison, Charles. *How to Help Your Gifted Child.* New York: Monarch Press, 1970.

Gold, Milton. *Education of the Intellectually Gifted.* Columbus, Ohio: Charles E. Merrill, 1965.

Gowan, John, and Bruch, Catherine. *The Academically Talented Student and Guidance.* Boston: Houghton Mifflin Co., 1971.

Gowan, John; Khatena, J.; and Torrance, E. P., eds. *Educating the Ablest.* Itasca, Ill.: F. E. Peacock Publishing, 1979.

Guilford, J. P. *Intelligence, Creativity, and Their Educational Implications.* San Diego, Calif.: Robert Knapp, 1968.

Hunkins, Francis P. *Involving Students in Questioning.* Boston: Allyn and Bacon, 1976.

Kaplan, Sandra. *Providing Programs for the Gifted and Talented: A Handbook.* Reston, Va.: Council for Exceptional Children, 1975.

Kaufmann, Felice. *Your Gifted Child and You.* Reston, Va.: Council for Exceptional Children, 1976.

Krathwohl, D. R.; Bloom, B. S.; and Masia, B. B. *Taxonomy of Educational Objectives. Handbook 2: Affective Domain.* New York: David McKay, 1964.

Labuda, Michael, ed. *Creative Reading for Gifted Learners: A Design for Excellence.* Newark, Del.: International Reading Association, 1974.

Lyon, H. "Education of the Gifted and Talented." *Exceptional Children* 43, no. 3 (1976): 166–67.

Maker, C. June. *Providing Programs for the Gifted Handicapped.* Reston, Va.: Council for Exceptional Children, 1977.

_____. *Training Teachers for the Gifted and Talented: A Comparison of Models.* Reston, Va.: Council for Exceptional Children, 1975.

Martinson, R. A. "Research on the Gifted and Talented: Its Implication for Education." In *Education of the Gifted and Talented: Report to the Congress of the United States by the U.S. Commissioner of Education.* Washington, D.C.: Government Printing Office, 1972.

_____, and Seagoe, May V. *The Abilities of Young Children*. Reston, Va.: Council for Exceptional Children, 1967.

Meeker, M. *Advance Teaching Judgment, Planning, and Decision Making*. El Segundo, Calif.: SOI Institute, 1976.

_____. *A Beginner's Reader About Guilford's Structure of the Intellect*. El Segundo, Calif.: SOI Institute, 1974.

Mirman, N. "Teacher Qualifications for Educating the Gifted." *Gifted Child Quarterly* 8, no. 3 (1964): 123–26.

Nolte, Jane. "Nearly...Everything You've Always Wanted to Know About the Gifted and Talented." Wauwatosa, Wisconsin, Council for the Gifted and Talented, 1976.

Ray, J. *Turning On Bright Minds*. Houston: Prologues, 1977.

Renzulli, Joseph S. *The Enrichment Triad Model*. Mansfield Center, Conn.: Creative Learning Press, 1977.

_____. *A Guide for Evaluating Programs for the Gifted and Talented*. Reston, Va.: Council for Exceptional Children, 1975.

_____, and Smith, Linda H. *A Guidebook for Developing Individualized Education Programs (IEP) for Gifted and Talented Students*. Mansfield Center, Conn.: Creative Learning Press, 1979.

Sanders, Norris M. *Classroom Questions, What Kinds?* New York: Harper and Row, 1966.

Stanley, Julian C.; Keating, D. P.; and Fox, L. *Mathematical Talent: Discovery, Description, and Development*. Baltimore: Johns Hopkins Press, 1974.

Star Power: Providing for the Gifted and Talented. Instructional Services, Region 13 Education Service Center, 7703 North Lamar, Austin, Texas 78752.

Syphers, Dorothy F. *Gifted and Talented Children: Practical Programming for Teachers and Principals*. Reston, Va.: Council for Exceptional Children, 1972.

Torrance, E. Paul. *Guiding Creative Talent*. New York: Drieger, 1976.

_____. *Discovery and Nurturance of Giftedness in the Culturally Different*. Reston, Va.: Council for Exceptional Children, 1977.

Treffinger, Donald J., and Curl, Clifford D. *Self-Directed Study Guide on the Education of the Gifted and the Talented*. Ventura, Calif.: Office of Ventura County Superintendent of Schools, 1976.

142

Tuckman, Bruce Wayne. *Evaluating Instructional Programs.* Rockleigh, N.J.: Allyn and Bacon, 1979.

Tuttle, Frederick B., Jr. *Gifted and Talented Students.* Rev. ed. Washington, D.C.: National Education Association, 1983.

Williams, Frank E. *A Total Creativity Program for Individualizing and Humanizing the Learning Process.* Englewood Cliffs, N.J.: Educational Technology Publications, 1972.

Periodicals

Dromenon
Box 2244
New York, NY 10011

Education Unlimited
1834 Meetinghouse Road
Boothwyn, PA 19061

Exceptional Children
Council for Exceptional Children
1920 Association Drive
Reston, VA 22091

G/C/T
350 Weinacker Avenue
Mobile, Al 36604

Gifted Child Newsletter
RD #1, Box 128-A
Egg Harbor Road
Sewell, NJ 08080

Gifted Child Quarterly
4175 Lovell Road, Suite 140
Circle Pines, MN 55014

Gifted International
College of Education
University of South Florida
Tampa, FL 33620

Journal of Creative Behavior
Creative Educational Foundation, Inc.
State University College
1300 Elmwood Avenue
Buffalo, NY 14222

Journal for the Education of the Gifted
Council for Exceptional Children
1920 Association Drive
Reston, VA 22091

National/State Leadership Training Institute on the Gifted and the Talented *Bulletin*
One Wilshire Building
624 South Grand Avenue
Los Angeles, CA 90017

Roeper Review
Roeper City and County Schools
2190 North Woodward
Bloomfield Hills, MI 48013

Media

Simple Gifts (videotapes)
University of Wisconsin Telecommunications Center
WHA-TV
Madison, WI 53706

Talks with Teachers about Gifted and Talented Students:
   Initiating a Program
   Teacher Selection and Program Evaluation
   Training Teachers to Work with Gifted Learners
   Funding
   Parents of the Gifted and Talented: A Teacher's View
   A Parent's View of Gifted and Talented Children
     (audiotapes)
NEA Professional Library
1201 16th Street, NW
Washington, DC 20036

Threat or Invitation: Program Development for Gifted and Talented (videotape by Frederick B. Tuttle, Jr., and Laurence A. Becker) Educational Communications Center State University of New York, College at Brockport Brockport, NY 14420

Associations

American Association for Gifted Children
15 Gramercy Park
New York, NY 10003
(212) 473-4266

The Association for the Gifted (TAG)
Council for Exceptional Children
1920 Association Drive
Reston, VA 22091
(703) 620-3660

Mensa Gifted Children Program
John B. Ceccherelli, National Coordinator
918 Forest Road
Endwell, NY 13760
(607) 748-7159

The National Association for Creative Children and Adults
8080 Springvalley Drive
Cincinnati, OH 45236
(513) 631-1777

National Association for Gifted Children
4175 Lovell Road, Suite 140
Circle Pines, MN 55014
(612) 784-3475

National Association of State Boards of Education
701 North Fairfax Street, Suite 340
Alexandria, VA 22314
(703) 684-4000

National/State Leadership Training Institute on the Gifted and the Talented
One Wilshire Building
624 South Grand Avenue
Los Angeles, CA 90017
(213) 489-7470

The World Council for Gifted and Talented Children, Inc.
Dorothy Sisk, Executive Secretary
College of Education
University of South Florida
Tampa, FL 33620
(813) 974-3638

ADDITIONAL RESOURCES FOR THE THIRD EDITION

A. *Advanced Learning Activities Program.* Warwick Public Schools, Warwick, R.I., 1982.

B. *AIP/TAG Advanced Skills Curriculum Activities Handbook II.* Boston Public Schools, District III/Boston College Collaborative, Spring 1982.

C. Callahan, Carolyn, et al. "Evaluating a Local Gifted Program: A LEA-University Cooperative Effort." 1980. ED 195 589

D. Clendening, Corinne. *Challenging the Gifted Curriculum: Enrichment and Acceleration Models.* New York: R. R. Bowker, 1983.

E. _____, and Davies, Ruth. *Creating Programs for the Gifted: A Guide for Teachers, Librarians, and Students.* New York: R. R. Bowker, 1980.

F. Cox, June; Daniel, Neil; and Boston, Bruce. *Educating Able Learners: Programs and Promising Practices.* Austin: University of Texas Press, 1985.

G. Gallagher, James J.; Weiss, Patricia; Oglesby, Krista; and Thomas, Tim. *Report on Education of Gifted, Volume I: Surveys of Education of Gifted Students.* Washington, D.C.: U.S. Office of Gifted and Talented, 1982.

H. *Gifted Child Quarterly* 26, no. 1, Winter 1982.

I. Jordan, June B., and Grossi, John A., eds. *An Administrator's Handbook on Designing Programs for the Gifted and Talented.* Reston, Va.: Council for Exceptional Children, 1980. Ed 196 179

J. Juntune, Joyce, ed. *Successful Programs for the Gifted and Talented.* St. Paul: National Association for Gifted Children, 1981.

K. Maker, C. June. *Critical Issues in Gifted Education.* Rockville, Md.: Aspen Systems, 1982.

L. _____. *Curriculum Development for the Gifted.* Rockville, Md.: Aspen Systems, 1982.

M. _____. *Teaching Models in the Education of the Gifted.* Rockville, Md.: Aspen Systems, 1982.

N.   Perrone, Phillip, and Male, Robert. *The Developmental Educator and Guidance of Talented Learners.* Rockville, Md.: Aspen Systems, 1981.

O.   Sellin, Donald F., and Berick, Jack W. *Educating Gifted and Talented Learners.* Rockville, Md.: Aspen Systems, 1980.

P.   *Talented and Gifted Programs: Curriculum Activities Handbook for TAG and AIP Classes.* Boston Public Schools, District III/Boston College Collaborative, Spring, 1981.

Q.   Treffinger, Donald. Editorial. *Gifted Child Quarterly* 26, no. 2, Spring 1982.

R.   _____. *Gifted Education with the Total School Program.* Buffalo, N.Y.: DOK Publishers, 1986.

ACTIVITIES FOR TEACHERS

PROGRAM DESIGN

Rationale

Need: Beside the characteristics, list some specific difficulties that may arise in a classroom. Add other characteristics and related problems.

Characteristics	Related Problems in School
• Divergent thinking ability	_____
	_____
• Highly verbal	_____
	_____
• Critical of self and others	_____
	_____
• Divergent modes of response	_____
	_____
• Persistent in pursuit of own goals	_____
	_____

Misconceptions and Concerns

List specific misconceptions and concerns that exist in your area. Beside each, outline a response.

Misconception or Concern	Reponse
(Example: The gifted can make it on their own.)	(Example: Some only doing mediocre work, others have emotional/defensive problems, only a few really achieving to potential ...)
_____	_____
_____	_____
_____	_____
_____	_____

_____   _____

_____   _____

_____   _____

_____   _____

Administrative Designs

For each of the following designs or program options, list arguments in favor (pro) of its use in your situation and arguments against (con).

Design	Pro	Con
Semiseparated	_____	_____
	_____	_____
Integrated	_____	_____
	_____	_____
Accelerated	_____	_____
	_____	_____
Enrichment	_____	_____
	_____	_____

Briefly describe a specific administrative design that might work in your situation (see Glossary of Administrative Designs on pp. 98–100).

_____

_____

_____

_____

After selecting a potential design for your situation, list as many factors as you can that will help you implement this design (e.g., interested teachers, concerned parents, historical precedence of support for students).

Positive (Facilitators)

_____

_____

_____

Now list all those factors that may impede implementation of this design (e.g., budget, transportation, lack of in-service).

Negative (Inhibitors)

_____

_____

_____

Check the most important inhibitors that have to be overcome before the program can be implemented. Discuss ways these problems may be overcome.

EXAMINATION OF CASE STUDY

Read the case study of Ralph on pp. 39–40. Using the modified problem-solving model that follows, discuss the questions about the case study. Try to be very specific in your responses. This examination may be facilitated by having several groups explore different questions and share the results.

Model

1. *Identify the problem.* State the specific problem implied in the question.

2. *Identify alternative solutions.* List as many possible solutions to the problem as you can.

3. *Evaluate the solutions.* Discuss each solution, considering both objective and subjective factors.

4. *Select the best alternative.*

Questions (For each of the situations, assume the school and the community are similar to your own.)

1. If you were Ralph's *parents*, what would you have done at each grade level? What would you do now?

2. If you were Ralph's *teachers*, what would you have done or suggested as a course of action for Ralph and his parents?

3. If you were the *principal* of Ralph's school, what would you have suggested for the boy? If you had several children like Ralph in your school, what would you do?

CURRICULAR MODELS

Bloom's Taxonomy

Select a specific concept or topic from your curriculum (e.g., a particular novel or scientific principle), and write specific activities for it within each of the following levels of the taxonomy:

Knowledge: _____

_____

_____

Comprehension: _____

_____

_____

Application: _____

_____

_____

Analysis: _____

_____

_____

Synthesis: _____

_____

_____

Evaluation: _____

_____

_____

Assume you are about to assess a classroom situation to determine whether or not the activities are at the higher levels of the taxonomy. What kinds of student behavior would you look for in this class? List three sample behaviors for each of the levels listed.

Application

(Example: Student applies knowledge to new situation.)

1. _____

2. _____

3. _____

Analysis

(Example: Student classifies main ideas and supporting details.)

1. _____

2. _____

3. _____

Synthesis

(Example: Student combines ideas from different sources and draws a conclusion.)

1. _____

2. _____

3. _____

Structure of the Intellect

Since this is a more complex area, a series of activities is included to help familiarize you with the components of the S.I. Model.*

1. Operation and Content

    1.1   Write the name of each incomplete figure on p. 155 on the lines below the items. This is an example of *Cognition* of *Figural, Symbolic,* and *Semantic* content.

    1.2   On a separate page recall as many of the items as you can. This is an example of *Recall* of *Figural, Symbolic,* and *Semantic* content.

    1.3   Divide this list into three subcategories. You should have groupings similar to *Figural* (pictures and shapes), *Symbols* (letters and numbers), and *Semantic* (words). This is an example of *Convergent Production.*

*Many of the activities in this section were developed by Donald Nasca, State University of New York, College at Brockport.

1.4 Using letters from words in list 1.2, construct as many words as you can. This is an example of *Divergent Production*.

1.5 Circle all words in your new list (1.4) with two or more vowels. This is an example of *Evaluation*.

2. Product

2.1 Invent a vegemal (a combination of a vegetable and an animal—e.g., carrophant—carrot and elephant). List several. Each vegemal is a *Unit*.

2.2 Group the vegemals into separate categories. Each category is a *Class*.

2.3 State the rationale (characteristic) for the groupings. The statement is a *Relationship*.

2.4 List the vegemals in hierarchical order so that you can add additional vegemals in appropriate positions. You now have a *System*.

2.5 Change some of the vegemals so that they would fit in a different position on your hierarchy. The new vegemals are *Transformations*.

2.6 Create some "What-would-happen-if . . ." questions and answer them. For example, what would happen if you mated a carrophant with an asperphant? You might have a carrot or an asperphant. The answer is an *Implication*.

Renzulli's Triad

In the spaces that follow, briefly outline a sample "Unit" in your specific area. (See sample given in Chapter 3).

Exploratory Activities (List materials and short activities you might use to interest your students in the topic.)

- _____

- _____

- _____

- _____

- _____

- _____

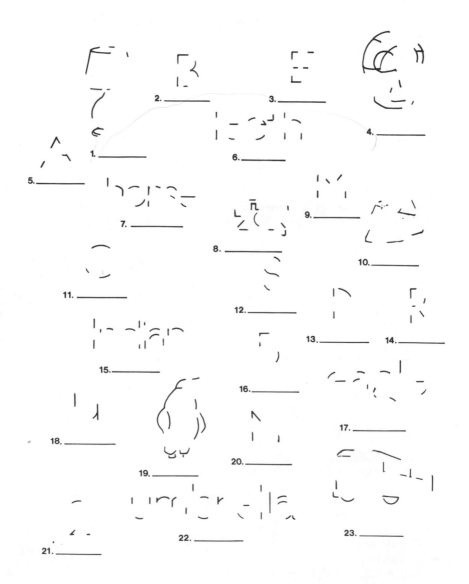

1. _____
2. _____
3. _____
4. _____
5. _____
6. _____
7. _____
8. _____
9. _____
10. _____
11. _____
12. _____
13. _____
14. _____
15. _____
16. _____
17. _____
18. _____
19. _____
20. _____
21. _____
22. _____
23. _____

NOTE: These drawings are used with the permission of Donald Nasca.

Training Activities (List the specific areas of skill development and describe one in detail.)

* _____

* _____

* _____

* _____

* _____

* _____

Possible Investigations (List some possible extensions of the theme students might wish to pursue in depth. Beside each possibility, cite a potential "real" audience.)

Problem	*Audience*
_____	_____
_____	_____
_____	_____

TEACHER SELECTION

1. From the following list, check those teacher characteristics that you feel would be most appropriate for your program. Then discuss them with the group.

   * highly intelligent
   * friendly
   * flexible and creative
   * demanding
   * self-confident and emotionally mature
   * sense of humor
   * interested in many areas
   * knowledgeable in subject area
   * experienced in system
   * businesslike in classroom behavior

- in favor of special provisions for gifted students
- hard grader
- alert
- well trained to work with the gifted and talented
- extremely professional in attitude and actions
- intellectually honest
- nonauthoritarian
- enthusiastic

The traits cited are not unique to the teacher of the gifted. Indeed most would be valuable characteristics for any teacher. However, some of these, such as self-confidence and high intelligence, are particularly important in classes for gifted because of the intellectual challenge presented by these students.

2. Write the teacher characteristics your group feels appropriate on the following lines.

A. _____   G. _____

B. _____   H. _____

C. _____   I. _____

D. _____   J. _____

E. _____   K. _____

F. _____   L. _____

3. Prioritize the characteristics by placing the representative letters on the appropriate lines in the sorting pyramid.

Most Vital	Vital	Somewhat Vital	Less Vital	Least Vital

4. List the characteristics considered *somewhat vital*, *vital*, and *most vital* on the following lines and write two indicative behaviors for each.

4.1 _____

    4.11 _____

    4.12 _____

4.2 _____

    4.21 _____

    4.22 _____

4.3 _____

    4.31 _____

    4.32 _____

4.4 _____

    4.41 _____

    4.42 _____

4.5 _____

    4.51 _____

    4.52 _____

4.6 _____

    4.61 _____

    4.62 _____

4.7 _____

    4.71 _____

    4.72 _____

4.8 _____

    4.81 _____

    4.82 _____

5. As a group compile a checklist of teacher behaviors that might help locate a qualified teacher of gifted and talented.

_____

_____

_____

_____

_____

_____

_____

_____

_____

EVALUATION

Development of Questions

List the major goals of the progam in the column at the left and the questions that might be asked about each goal in the column at the right.

Goals	*Questions*
(Example: Students will work at the higher levels of the taxonomy.)	(Example: Did the classroom activity reflect work at the higher levels of the taxonomy? Did student products demonstrate ability to synthesize and evaluate ideas?)
_____	_____
_____	_____
_____	_____
_____	_____

Categorize the questions, writing more encompassing ones where necessary.

Questions	Instruments/Methods
(Example: Did the classroom activity reflect work at the higher levels of the taxonomy?)	(Example: Classroom observation using the Florida Taxonomy of Cognitive Behavior)

_____

_____

_____

_____

_____

_____

_____

_____

_____